I0160405

THE KUNDALINI YOGA
CHRISTIAN MASTER
IS

BOOK FOUR OF " THE HIDDEN MASTER " SERIES

BOOK ONE OF " THE HIDDEN MASTER " SERIES

BAPTIST GNOSTIC CHRISTIAN EUBONICKUNDALINI SPIRITUAL KI DO HERMENEUTIC METAPHYSICS

ISBN-10: 0595206786 & ISBN-13: 978-0595206780

BOOK TWO OF " THE HIDDEN MASTER " SERIES

CHRISTIAN KUNDALINI SCIENCE- PROOF OF THE SOUL- CRYPTOGRAM SOLUTION OF EGYPTIAN STELA 55001-&

OPENING THE HOOD OF RA

ISBN: 9780578100791

BOOK THREE OF " THE HIDDEN MASTER " SERIES

TRAPEZIUM GIZA PYRAMID ARTIFICIAL BLACK HOLE THEORY

ISBN: 978-1-300-87497-3

ALL SO

THE 20 PENNIES A DAY DIET PLAN

ISBN: 9781300270089

BY FRANK M. CONAWAY, JR.

ISBN: 978-1-312-33119-8

THE KUNDALINI YOGA CHRISTIAN MASTER IS

ISBN: 978-1-312-33119-8

FRANK M. CONAWAY, JR.

FRANK M. CONAWAY, JR.

FRANK M. CONAWAY, JR.

FRANK M. CONAWAY, JR.

FRANK M. CONAWAY, JR.

THE KUNDALINI

YOGA:

CHRISTIAN

MASTER IS ME

KUNDALINI MASTER YOGI

THERE MAY BE A QUESTION AS TO WHY AM I SAYING " CHRISTIAN " IN RELATION TO THE TERM " KUNDALINI MASTER ". LOOK AT ALL OF THE INTERNET SITES WHERE PEOPLE ARE TALKING ABOUT THE KUNDALINI SUBJECT. IT'S HARD TO TELL WHO KNOWS WHAT THEY ARE TALKING ABOUT, VERSES THE PEOPLE WHOM JUST DON'T HAVE A CLUE! SOMETIMES THE ONLY ANSWER TO SOME OF THE REDERIC IS TO SUMMONS " LIGHT ". THIS IS PART OF THE REASON THAT I AM WRITING ABOUT THE SUBJECT.

WHO IS THE KUNDALINI MASTER?

IN THE MOVIE " THE LAST DRAGON ", SURE NUFF ASKS BRUCE LEE ROY AS TO WHO THE MASTER " **IS** "? I'M NOT GOING TO GET CAUGHT IN THAT TRAP < MAN >, BUT I CAN GIVE YOU A ANSWER: " IT IS ME "! < JUST INCASE YOU THINK THAT I HAVE ANSWERED THIS QUESTION POORLY, PLEASE NOTE THAT I DID NOT USE THE TETRAGRAMATION < WHICH WOULD BE " I AM " >. AH HA, SO ENDITH THE TRICK! >

ALL YOU REALLY CARE ABOUT

ALL YOU REALLY CARE ABOUT IS TWO THINGS. IF YOU ARE CHASING " THE KUNDALINI ", ALL YOU CARE ABOUT IS TWO THINGS. YOU REALLY SHOULD CARE ABOUT MORE THAN THAT. 1) YOU NEED TO KNOW WHAT THE PROCESS OF THE INVOKATION IS – HOW TO START THE KUNDALINI COIL TO FIRE. 2) WHAT TO EXPECT DURING THE KUNDALINI EXPERIENCE – WHAT CAN HAPPEN. 3) HOW TO EXIT FROM THE KUNDALINI SEQUENCE – TO CLOSE THE ACTIVATED COIL. I BELIEVE THAT I HAVE COVERED NUMBERS 1 AND 3 IN MY OTHER WRITINGS, IT IS NUMBER 2 THAT I DID NOT FULLY DISCRIBE. TO HEAR SOME OF OTHER PEOPLES COMMENTS ON THE KUNDALINI EXPERIANCE SUBJECT SURE HAS BEEN FUNNY I MIGHT ADD!

FINAL IS NOT KUNDALINI

" WHAT IS THIS TO US " < I HAD TO ADD THIS FOR THE CHRISTIAN MINDSET >? I HAD TO ADD THIS BECAUSE IT IS A " MEANS " OF STOP FOR THE TRUE STUDENT OF THE INFINITE. THE TRUE STUDENT OF THE INFINITE MAY FIND THEMSELVES UNABLE TO LEAVE " THE STUDENT

MINDSET " WHEN THEY HAVE BEEN STUDYING ON WHAT COULD BE CALLED " THE INFINITE TRUTH ". THE STUDENT MAY KEEP FINDING NEW SUBJECTS RELATED TO THEIR SUBJECT OF STUDY. THIS STATE OF MIND IS REFERED TO AS BEING LOCKED. TO EXPLAIN A LITTLE ABOUT THE MINDSET CALLED LOCKED, I WOULD LIKE TO SAY A FEW THINGS. THE LOCKED MINDSET COULD BE DRIVEN BY WHAT COULD BE CALLED AN ADDICTION. IT WOULD SEEM AS IF THE MIND CAN ENTER INTO THE "PLEASURE PRINCIPUL " OVER ANY SUBJECT. JUST BECAUSE A PERSON ENTERS INTO AN " ADDICTED MIND SET ", THAT DOES NOT SAY THAT THE PERSON IS OVER POWERED BY THEIR ACTIONS. LET'S LOOK AT ADDICTION ANOTHER WAY FOR AN MINUTE. DO PEOPLE LIKE TO DO THINGS THAT THEY LIKE TO DO? SURPOSE A PERSON DOES WHAT THEY LIKE TO DO WITHOUT HURTING ANYONE ELSE, IS THAT ACTIVITY THAT BRINGS THE PERSON JOY WRONG? WHAT BUSINESS IS IT OF YOURS WHAT A PERSON DOES WITH THEIR LIFE? I MEAN " REALLY "!/? SOMETIMES PEOPLE JUST WANT TO DO WHAT THEY WANT TO DO. I COULD GO FUTHER, BUT I THINK THAT ENDS THE NEED FOR COMMENT.

FROM THE AUTHOR OF: BAPTIST GNOSTIC CHRISTIAN

EUBONIC KUNDALINI SPIRITUAL KI DO HERMENEUTIC

METAPHYSICS ISBN #0595206780

WIKIPEDIA ON THESE

ALBERT EINSTEIN'S BRAIN

ALTER EGO

ALTERED STATE OF CONSCIOUSNESS

ALTRUISM

CADUCEUS

DIMETHYLTRYTAMINE < DMT >

DOUBLE ENTENDRE

EURECKIA

GEHENNA

ISOLATION TANK

PINEAL GLAND

PSYCHOSOMATIC

PYRE

OVAL

SENSORY DEPRIVATION

SLEEP DEPRIVATION

TESTICLE < TESTIS, DIMINUTIVE OF TESTIS, MEANING " WITNESS < CHECK ALSO BLUELETTERBIBLE > " OF VIRILITY,   PLURAL TESTES >

YOGA

FRANK M. CONAWAY, JR.

KUNDALINI YOGA WARNING

As I understand it, Kundalini Yoga is the highest form of the yoga sciences. There is a reason that there is a spiritual part of the training. The warnings given by the yoga masters are not to be taken lightly! So you can understand what you are dealing with, you are attempting an controlled " near death experience " that may include the release of dimethyltrytamine from the pineal gland. That is just the end of the story!

POSSIBLE TITLES < THESE ARE TITLES THAT I HAVE GONE THRU IN WORKING ON THIS DOCUMENT >:

KUNDALINI YOGA: CHRISTIAN MASTER

MASTER OF CHRISTIAN KUNDALINI YOGA

SPIRITUAL SHOCK: KUNDALINI CALL OUT- THE FINAL CRACKDOWN

NATIVES OR INDIGENOUS PEOPLE OF THE AMERICAS

REWRITE HISTORY

INDIGENOUS PEOPLE BUILT THE GREAT PYRAMID: REWRITE HISTORY

MAYBE THE PEOPLE BEFORE ADAM KADMON

OLD WORLD ORDER

WHO'S TEMPLE KNOWLEDGE

THE MISSING KEY: REWRITE HISTORY

EXPLAIN THIS

MASTER OF KUNDALINI

KUNDALINI OF THE REVELATION

FRANK M. CONAWAY, JR.

EGYPTIAN GONE

I had left Egypt for the final time after I finished CHRISTIAN KUNDALINI SCIENCE-PROOF OF THE SOUL- CRYPTOGRAM SOLUTION OF EGYPTIAN STELA 55001- & OPENING THE HOOD OF RA ISBN# 978-0-578-10079-1. That is what I thought. I came across a new kundalini book of which I asked myself if this author had opened the kundalini coil, or was he just writing about things that had been written about several times before? I took note of this, but it did not bother me to the point where I wanted to write about it! He commented on a lot of topics related to metaphysics that I had explored, but they were not of any major concern to me. Follow me please as I move slowly to the point of why I am writing again. I was done " my " work, whew! I was leaving Egypt, great. I could see the forest again and not trees. That was great. Then it happened again. A load of relevant knowledge was dropped in my lap so to speak. It was so powerful that I had to come back. This time I won't be talking about a tree, but this time I will be talking about the whole forest. What was it that I was dealing with when I wrote TRAPEZIUM GIZA PYRAMID ARTIFICIAL BLACK HOLE THEORY ISBN# 978-1-300-87497-3? I just saw a publication that stated that "what is now being called a black hole may be a black star ". I was speaking of a structure that was an energy generator / collector. I need to move on for now. < Added later: What I came across was so powerful that it caused this session of writing. Really two things happened at the same time. The first was the knowledge of "The Code 2000 "some 13 years later and why? The second reason is found at the later clue of the serpent and the forest. >

MY WAY

I guess that in a way, I am writing my books for myself. There were things that I wanted / needed to know. I had wanted these things for myself. The great I wanted them! I had to know. I had to find out for myself. I had hoped to have been able to pass my work on to certain people, but maybe not. I guess in the long run that it doesn't matter anyway. It really doesn't matter what anybody but me thinks anyway. Maybe some things can't be passed on. What does it really mean when you had a great person in your family? Does it mean that you should be great? No, and not at all. As a matter of fact, that type of spotlight pressure could stifle your growth. Maybe a person should only be measured by themselves. The question is did "you" do the best that you could do working with what you have? When you have done the best that you can do, maybe the only thing that is left is the signs that you left along the way that read: " I was here! " Now that I think about it, that may be just fine for me. My signs say: " I WAS HERE – FRANK – AKA FRANK JR. OF WHOM IS META 3.14! " What a sign. P.S. Take them to the Dojo – FRANK, my mans. Oh yah! Wow, that only leaves the sign.

THIS DOCUMENT STYLE

I do understand that you may look at the text in this document and wonder about the " style " that is being used. Many concepts that I discuss may be foreign to you. This is why I sometimes show research. I know that the way to do this is to give you the references and let you look them up yourself. I feel that in the long run, this way of recording this is best for you and I. I will try to take out as much as possible, but you have to think of this document as if you were doing research. While I might give you internet and YouTube examples, I feel that books and graphs are still the best way to " see " the transitions between the elements. In this way, you can lay your work out like a puzzle. Films and movies seem to be the best way to consume large amounts of information. The problem with this is that you need to know how what you consume is connected. Let me put this concept to you another way. Pick five different books from five different subjects. Read the five books. Now what you have is five different fragments of information in your mind. Science now knows that information makes paths in your brain. Yes like Swiss cheese. In the case that we are using, our Swiss cheese block would have five different holes or bubbles in it. You might not see the bubbles that represent pockets of information until you open or cut the cheese block. You might want to look up National Geographic: The New Science of the Brain in the February 2014 issue. There are two comments that I would like to record. First, on page 39: " The Glow Of Memory – When you form a memory, ' there's a physical change in the brain,' says Don Arnold, of the University of South California. Red and green dots on the branches extending from this rat neuron show where it contacts other neurons. As the rat forms new memories, new dots appear and old ones vanish." Second, on page 34: " The Color Of Thought – The brain's many regions are connected by some 100,000 miles of fibers called white matter – enough to circle the Earth four times. " This is what happens in the brain. This type of learning is called unformatted. The term unformatted in this case refers to there being no apparent link between the subjects. In a way it is like having a lot of programs on your computer that take up hard drive space and chew up memory by starting when you turn your computer on. We generally call this to make the computer " slow ". In reality the computer is not running slow, but the computer is performing the many tasks you asked it to do at start up. This very same thing can happen to the mind. As you might know, the mind searches itself when confronted with problems. Sometimes under great stress, the mind will rapidly access all of its know information to find a answer. The result of the mind accessing a lot of non related information can be a type of mental overload called confusion. When this happens, one can be said to be " lost " in one's own mind. Think of it as if someone changed the icons for the programs on your computer. What I am saying is if you had a typing program icon on a music program and didn't know it. Think of how much pressure you would be under if you had to find the program you need quickly. You start clicking on icon after icon opening programs. You rush as you try to close programs while opening others. Don't do it on your main computer, but you might want to try opening multiple programs on your old computer to see what happens. You might even want to time how long it takes the computer to finish working. Your computer may become busy. This is what happens when a person gets lost in their mind, which is not the same as " to have lost one's mind ". A researcher can become lost in their work by being overloaded or flooded with information. When dealing with a large complex subject like The Bible, it is very easy to get side tracked and then lost. I am " getting lost " right now because I moved away from the subject of the topic. I want to tell you something. If you use note cards or write the subject next to the word topic, you can keep track of your place. The second thing is that you might want to set a timer for every so often so that you can stretch. You might find that you can study for several hours in the same position. This might help you to not get so stiff. The way that The Bible is written, it takes a direct path from Eden thru The Fall of Man to Heaven. The Bible mentions several different topics that you could go off on in research. You must remember your main objective. I should tell you this, the world is designed to side track a person. The world can cause a person to " sleep walk " unto the crypt. What do I mean by that? In many cases people don't wary about an " after life " until they perceive that their life span is just about over. That is not what The Bible tells a person to do. The Bible suggests that a person should store their rewards in Heaven where man can't steal them.

SPIRITUAL PENITENTIARY JAILBIRDS

Let's cut right to the problem at hand. The Bible states that all < Adamic not others < giants >> man has fallen from grace due to the fall of Adam. We don't really have to look at the situation this way. We can say that there is something called " The fruit of everlasting life ". This was the food that man was suppose to consume. Man was cut off from this fruit of immortality. This is the quest! This is the business of the soul. Now the soul is encased in flesh. Think of your body, the flesh as being one of those " black and white " jail bird suites. When you see someone with one of those suites on, what do you think? You think that the person just escaped from JAIL! I know you are asking what do I mean? What does it mean when you see your fellow man? It means that you / we all are " spiritual jailbirds ". The main way out of the / this penitentiary is thru " the door called Death "! Death is sometimes called The Gates.

WHO IS GOING TO TELL YOU

Maybe some people have been aware of this and I just didn't hear them talk about it. I'm talking about the special rewards mentioned in The Book Of The Revelation. Maybe it's alright to just try to go to Heaven. Why would these special rewards not be talked about? I want to say the ego. I am relating the ego to " the desire of the self ". Can you just imagine people telling you about how you can win and they feeling that they want to win? It's what people talk about when they say " crabs in a bucket ". This might be really a form of human nature. There could be two periods or phases in which the human may have to deal with sharing this information. The first phase is when the person who knows is still an active " player ". This is to say that a person might not share this information with other people because " someone else might beat them to the **PRISE < PRYSE >** "! That seems like a valid reason not to share information with others. This brings me to asking myself why has a certain group said anything about this? Would the ego tell a person of a certain order that if a person is not of their order, then that person is not worthy of the **prize**! I might not understand this type of thought pattern due to my martial training. In thinking about that comment, there are two types of martial arts teachers. One teacher never wants to see their student exceed them. What can you say about that? You see this all the time in the martial arts movies. Sometimes the teacher would even harm the student to try to " **stifle** " the students progress. Now that I think about it, I don't know why I seem so surprised. I know a martial arts teacher like that! That is a very sad thing to say. Not really, that is just how that person is. On the other hand, there are teachers whom believe that their students should be better than them. This type of teacher can run into their own type of problem. I saw this type of situation for myself. The instructor spends years helping and teaching the student. The instructor might take the student from being a dud to being a " gifted " martial artist. Have you seen a martial arts movie where the student betrays the instructor after the instructor is out of their prime? I'm saying that the young student looks down on their instructor due to the instructor aging! This is called that the student has a lack of **loyalty**. This is a **personal** problem of the student. In a way, this is a double problem. The first problem is the inner attitude of the student. The second problem is that the student didn't learn the lessons about **loyalty and respect**. I want to say that I guess that it works itself out in the end. If you take this to the spiritual level, it seems; no, The Bible speaks about people like this and their relationship to GOD. Now how do I make this circle complete? Here we go back to The Garden of Eden.

MAN KNOW THYSELF

I think that you should now look up " man know thyself " and " know thyself " on the internet. The question that comes to mind at this point is did Adam know that he was created by GOD? Did Adam know who GOD is? Did Adam know about the nature of Satan? Maybe Adam didn't know about Satan and that's why Satan came within the Serpent or Snake. As I understand it, Adam gave the animals their names. I think the animals names tells something about the nature of the animal thru the " meanings " of the Hebrew letters. I guess this is the beginning of the inner learning of the Jewish system called " **Kabala** ". We don't have to ask if GOD knew that Adam was going to " transgress "! There are other books that describe how extremely sorry Adam was after being kicked out of The Garden of Eden. In a way The Bible could be called " the training book of Adam ". I guess that the question now is " did Adam know himself "? Strange, under the images there is a page with a bust of Pythagoras and the quote: " Man know thyself; then thou shalt know the Universe and God ". Another page says: " DNA – Divine Natural Attributes – Know Thyself – People Suffer For Lack Of Knowledge ". What about this one: " A psychopath is a person who has no regard for the pain of others, who is only concerned about getting their own desires fulfilled. As such all of humanity are psychopaths considering what we accept and allow on this earth " written by Anna Brix Thonsen. There is another quote of " Man know thyself; then thou shalt know the Universe and God " but attributed to the Temple of Apollo At Delphi. There are more, I must record this one. The image is of the book " Know Thyself ": Plato's First Alcibiades and Commentary. There is a image of a owl with the letters " AOL ". " The body is the house of god. Man, know thyself…And thou shalt know God ". There are a lot of interesting images. Now to show you how to get off track, one page said " Is planet Nibiru planet Christ ?"

WATER

I need to speak about the " topic related to metaphysics " as I stated. Let's start with talking about plain old " water ". You know what I mean when I say water don't you? Good. I am speaking of regular water that humans can drink. This is where the trees close in on your studies. Let me explain. Our topic is " plain old ' water ' ". Here we go!

WATER FALLS

Let's start talking about plane old water < this is the topic > which expands to: 1) Ph water values, 2) acid water, 3) alkaline water, 4) spring water, 5) distilled water, 6) fresh water, 7) sea water, the spin rate of the water, 8) mineral water, 9) magnetic water, 10) snow mountain water, 11) water from limestone, 12) crystal water, and 13) healing hot spring water. This last type of water leads us to our next topic.

WHO KNEW THIS

We knew this, who? This is how I would like to introduce the next body of knowledge " THE CODE " by CARL MUNCK. I would like to start with Disk 3. Hi back to you Carl < The Guide To The Past >. He wants to take the viewer back to Guatemala because he has something for " your " memory! The after that " we " will take a look at the lost continents, and even a peek at " The Bermuda Triangle "! The projected image says " **THE CODE 2000** by CARL MUNCK "! The current standard date time is August 02, 2013, therefore this was " known " thirteen years ago! Wow!!! It's like " Party Like It's 1999!" Look at these " crazy " numbers: 2160, 54, 8, 144, 5, 3, 180, 314, 432, 96, 360, 78, 2, 3, and 59: what is he talking about? Why is the geometry " L " there? Carl said: In my previous video, I introduced The Magnificent Code System involving the worlds Pyramids, Mounds, Maps, and Numbers. He states that these elements are a part of a system that is hidden! He also states that " The Order is arranged to confuse The Undisciplined Mind. The KEY to that was numbers! " He says that most people don't like numbers, but the undisciplined mind can " **make up false values for found values** ". Hence, I now believe that this is the Doctor Joyce Brothers experiment from Candied Camera in reverse! It could be where one can " see " a truth that is not understood and < project > believe to have not " seen " the reality for what it is!

ENTER THE ARCHAEOCRYPTOGRAPHER

Carl talks about the 144 relationship between The Bent Pyramid and The El Kula Pyramid. He notes that the figure 144 is thought to refer to " Light " in the geomantra science. He refers to the number 432 < 144 times 3 > and its relationship to The False Pyramid at Nadom Egypt. He talks about the good reason why to establish the musical frequency of " A " at 440 hertz rather than 432 hertz < vibrations per second >. He speaks about the potential damage to existing structures if this frequency was used. He commented on how certain types of music could have an awful effect. I thought that in the concept of the holographic universe that it could be this shift in standard that may actually be causing all of this global discord. As a matter of fact, I had assumed that it was a shift in frequency that was causing discord at the base kundalini chakra leading to all sorts of other problems. He explains the number 96 as relating to temple one at Tikal Guatemala called The Temple of The Giant Jaguar. < This is how I became drawn back to writing this. I later show you a piece of mail that I sent to the author about his new book, and asking if he was saying that he had completed the kundalini exercise. I was walking through a supermarket when I saw the National Geographic Expeditions magazine "mysteries of the maya – the rise, glory and collapse of an ancient civilization dated display until 9/6/13. The front cover is said to be a picture of " the pyramid known as El Castillo, or ' the castle, ' scrapes the sky at Chichen Itza in south Mexico. With staircases on each of its four sides and a temple at the top, the monument unites the Maya's soaring achievements in architecture and astronomy. At the spring and fall equinoxes, the setting sun casts serpent-like shadows along the northern stairs. " The rear cover is said to show " the towering Temple of the Great Jaguar dwarfs the surrounding jungle in Tikal, Guatemala". I opened the magazine and there it was again. This will be the third time that I have ciphered King Pakal's sarcophagus which is partially shown on page 65 of this magazine. The magazine claims that the image is of King Pakal being shown to be in the underworld. It is said to have been discovered in 1952. I had seen the image a few years ago and had ciphered it, but I never felt really satisfied until now. Back to our story. > He talks about a global pyramid matrix. He continues to explain pyramid structures in North and South America as being mathematically related to each other. The key he explains is the use of spherical mathematics to relate these global temples to each other. He goes on to add The Temple of The Masks to his " Earth History " grid map. He states that back in 1882 a ship named The Jesuman came in contact with a structure in the ocean at 28 degrees 40 minutes west of Greenwich; which converts to **59 degrees 48 minutes west** < check > of Giza on original maps. He states that Tikal temples 1 and 2 refer to longitudes; but temple 5 refers to latitude. He moves on to a site in Bolivia called The Gate of the Sun. If you look at the artwork carefully, one could conceive two inner birds on the face drawing forming a center point like pot or vase, with an outer bird being implied also. The whole scene could be considered as a glyphic code for The Kundalini Science in another culture. Carl goes into a science called **Palieomagnatism**. He then records: 1) the current Earth pole was from 12,000 years ago to today, 2) before that 18,000 to 48,000 years ago the Earth pole was at **Akpatok** Islands, 3) before that the pole was located in the **Greenland Sea** from 54,000 to 80,000 years ago, then 4) from 86,000 to 120,000 years ago at **Yukon**. He adds China's pyramid field to his ancient global matrix concept. His next global relationship is between Tiahuanaco, Xian, and The Lemirian Ruins which are said to be near Okinawa. < **Check James Churchwood** > From here he moves on to Giza and Easter Island. He makes special note of something called The Great Triangle. I think it should be called " The Great Triangles or Compasses " which he numbers as " 8 : 5 : and 2 = 0.8 " . I hope Carl will not be mad at me, but I must speak about his work. It is a given that a triangle is an three sided object that contains corner angles that total 180 degrees. This " double " triangle contains 360 degrees. He goes back to 0.8 times 360 degrees of form < gave us those numbers of 8, 5, and 2 >; 0.8 times 360 degrees becomes 288 times the 60 degrees corners in the triangle equal 17,280 which is encoded in the latitude of The Great Triangle which is 14 degrees 41 minutes 30.104 south latitude; which is 17,280 times 3 which equals 51,840 which encodes 106 degrees 15 minutes 32.603 seconds West of Giza. Is this a so called " Space Bass "? Carl calls this The Rosetta Stone of The Spherical Earth Grid! He has so much more that he talks about! He goes on to comment on personal " attitude and the results when using Pyramid Power or Universal Constant Power! "

WHAT INDIGENOUS PEOPLE

Our book search might as well as start here. Maybe we can find images of different peoples of the world. If we go to " EGYPT on The Potomac " by Anthony Browder we can find some images. On pages 62 – 63 the images of " 33 races " and names are listed. I might as well as list the names: 1), oh never mind. I guess I might as well: Russian Slav, 2) Blonde European, 3) Brunette European, 4) Modern Greek, 5) Persian, 6) Cirassian, 7) Hindoo, 8) Hungarian, 9) Semite, 10) Arab, 11) Turk, 12) Modern Egyptian, 13) Abyssinian, 14) Malay, 15) Polynesian, 16) Australian, 17) Negrito, 18) Zulu, 19) Papuan, 20) Soudan Negro, 21) Akka, 22) Fuegian, 23) Botocudo, 24) Pueblo Indian, 25) Esquimaux, 26) Plains Indian, 27) Samoyede, 28) Corean, 29) Japanese, 30) Aino, 31) Burmese, 32) Thibetan, and 33) Chinese. These head images are said to be on the Jefferson Library in Washington D. C.. I have seen them for myself. The book is available on my bookstore at spiritualshockbooks.com . It is stated that " contemporary biologists, anthropologists and geneticists now assert that humanity began in Africa and all humans evolved from them. The general consensus among scientists is that the emergence of ethnic variations of the original type took place between 50 – 30,000 years ago. An estimated timeline for this phenomena follows: Modern man, Homo Dapien Sapien, evolved entirely in Africa about 200,000 years ago; modern man came to occupy Asia at least 75,000 years ago; modern man came to occupy Western Asia (Europe) between 50 – 40,000 years ago. Contemporary scientists agree that " race " is an artificial construct that was created in order to declare one ethnic group superior to another based upon skin color. "

FRANK M. CONAWAY, JR.

FIRE FROM THE GODS: THE MYSTICAL TRANSIT

I have heard the phrase " fire from the Gods " used many times. I would just like to write the explanation that is given on page 60 of " EGYPT on The Potomac ". The subject is the Jefferson building. It is written: " the most visible aspect of the Jefferson Building is its copper-domed roof and the 23-karat gold-leafed Torch of Learning at its apex. The torch and dome rest on a rectangular building that spans two city blocks. Squares and rectangles are architectural shapes symbolizing the earth and man. Right angles do not exist in nature; they are man-made. Domes are all circular, and all reside in the dominion of the gods and goddesses. The torch symbolizes light and is a metaphor for knowledge, understanding, and wisdom. The placement of a dome on a rectangle is a symbolic act that represents ' bringing heaven to earth. ' Adding a torch to the dome represents the act of ' bringing the knowledge of heaven to earth. ' The fact that the torch and dome were placed in the center of the rectangle, over the main reading room, attests to the aim of the library's designers to make the knowledge of the universe available to all who have access to the library. " So here we have it stated that the fire of the gods is knowledge! Pages 52 – 53 tell the story in stone on the Adams Building of " the evolution of civilization and how it spread from East to the West. " There are currently questions about the time line of humans. In specific, there is a question of how the dates of The Bible can be related to the archeological data. If we stop thinking in this way, we can easily say that the biblical record is a sub record of what has taken place from creation to now. Really The Bible ends its record over one thousand years ago. In saying that I say that there is no conflict about what happened in ancient times. To put it another way, the dinosaur age had nothing to do with the time of the creation of the Adamic race. So the question is was there human proto types around during the time of the dinosaurs? I don't see why not, they say that they found the bones! In " EGYPT on The Potomac " on page 43 Anthony T. Browder writes: " it is surprising that so few people know that the Washington Monument, easily the most recognizable symbol of the United States, is actually a copy of a 6,000 year-old symbol that represents the resurrection of the first ruler of Ancient Egypt ".

ENTER THE OBELISK

Again referring to " EGYPT on The Potomac " on page 17 Anthony T. Browder writes " there were approximately 1200 tekhenwy built in Kemet in ancient times, but only about a dozen are found in Egypt today. Many of the tekhenwy removed from Egypt are now in Istanbul, London, Paris, Berlin, **New York**, Rome, Vatican City, and elsewhere throughout the world. The tekhenwy are now called obelisks by their new owners, and few know their origin or that they symbolize the resurrection of the African king Ausar. "

THE SETTING SUN

It is generally accepted that the Sun rises in the east and sets in the west. This is established in relation to how planet Earth is said to rotate and wobble. Referring again to " EGYPT on The Potomac " on page 17 Anthony T. Browder writes: " the Kemetic model for temple construction and orientation was replicated in the design of cathedrals and churches built throughout Europe during the Middle Ages. A properly constructed church was built on sacred ground with its entrance facing west and the Holy of Holies in the east, as were many solar temples in Kemet. " So here we have referenced that the temples before Christ faced the setting Sun. Again in " EGYPT on The Potomac " on page 44 Anthony T. Browder writes: " The Heru Bedhet inside the Washington Monument is silent testimony to the importance of Kemet in the minds and hearts of America's Founding Fathersvand designers of Washington, D. C.. " The Washington Monument has a base width of 55 feet and a height of 555 feet. It remains true to the proportions of tekhenwy in Kemetwith a ratio of ten times the base height. " Shown is a photograph with " The Heru inside the Washington Monument " written under it. The Heru Bedhet looks like a winged solar disk with a six pointed star in the middle and a serpent on each side.

THREE-FIFTHS MAN TAX

The article continues with: " It might be curious to some that all the Washington Monument's measurements bare in fives, specifically, five fives. We already know that the number five represents man, but those who are skeptical of this interpretation should read Article I, Section 2.3 of the U. S. Constitution which states: Representatives and direct Taxes shall be apportioned…according to their respective Numbers, which shall be determined by adding to the whole Number of free Persons…excluding Indians not taxed, [and] three-fifths of all other Persons. (Emphasis added). A simple translation of Article I, section 2.3 would read: Representatives to Congress and taxes shall be determined by census of free white males … and three-fifth of their slaves. Slavery was not mentioned in the U.S. Constitution, yet it existed, and enslaved Africans were referred to as " all other Persons. ' Although a reference to the number five representing man is not specifically mentioned in the **Constitution**, it is inferred by the statements, " whole Number of free Persons " and " three-fifth of all other Persons. ' Enslaved?

BROWDERS 666

In " EGYPT on The Potomac " on page 19 Anthony T. Browder writes about " THE SYMBOLIC USE OF NUMBERS ". The book states: " numbers are not just quantitative, they can also be qualitative and symbolic expressions of religious and philosophical ideas. Numbers are also important when analyzing buildings because the number and location of objects, such as doors, windows, and steps, have functional and symbolic value. " He goes on to give a " brief guide" " to the " symbolic meaning of a few numbers. " I would like to note what is said about the numbers five and six. " Five represents man. There are five parts of the human body (head, arms, and legs). Man has five fingers, five toes, and five senses. The word man literally means ' mind. ' It is derived from Sanskrit, and it has no sexual connotation. In this context, woman means the ' womb ' that produces man / mind. Six represents death. From the earliest times people were buried in a six-sided box (a coffin), were carried to their grave by six pallbearers, and were buried six feet under the earth. Symbolically, the number 666 refers to the death of the body, mind, and spirit of a person, and not the devil as is commonly believed. "

FRANK M. CONAWAY, JR.

THE STUDY OF LIGHT

Since I have reflected upon on what has been written about the Sun, obelisks, and the number 666; I would like to note one more thing before I move on to a joke. In " EGYPT on The Potomac " on page 18 Anthony T. Browder writes: " the word mason is derived from the Latin words mass and son. It literally means ' Child of Light," and expresses the desire to pursue ' light,' a metaphor for the sun that symbolizes knowledge. The term Child of Light was first used to identify students who had completed 42 years of study in the temples of Kemet." Is the concept of 42 years of study is something to laugh about?

THE OWLS OAK

The saying goes something like this: " a wise old owl stand on a oak, the more he heard the less he spoke" ! In " EGYPT on The Potomac " on page 68 Anthony T. Browder writes the " AFTERWORD: AN ANALYSIS OF THE CAPITOL GROUNDS ". Under the title, a map is shown. Under the map it says: " an owl image is visible in this 1874 landscaping plan for the Capitol grounds ". In comment it is written: " the lines of the sidewalks on the Capitol grounds form the image of an owl, the symbol of Minerva, Roman goddess of wisdom. This image establishes a clear link between knowledge and power, Congress and the library that serves it. " I would like to comment upon the owl. My joke has not too due with the owl of the Capitol grounds, but the " wise old owl and the oak ". The owl is wise because it can turn its head around 360 degrees. That means that the owl " can see " everything. Mr. Browder has already made the owl and wisdom connection. What is a oak tree? A oak is a very strong tree. From Wikipedia we find " in spring, a single oak tree produces both male flowers (in the form of catkins) and small female flowers. The fruit is a nut called an acorn. " From this it seems that it could be said the oak tree is like or symbolic of Adam Kadmon. The tree is him, her, them. Plus, the tree has nuts. People often think of soft money as being made of paper. Hard coin money makes a lot of noise; verses the more soft money that you have stacked up, the less sound that it makes even in the wind. It is well known that paper can be made of wood. So now we are looking for the owl oak paper money connection. Pull out a dollar bill. Look Washington in the face. Fold the dollar bill in half. The half way line should extend above Washington's head next to the second " T " in the word STATES under the word reserve. To your right is the number 1. Use a straight edge to make a line across STATES OF AMERICA. The line should just be over top of the number 1. Move backward away from the number 1 just a little towards the word AMERICA. Stop when you get to the curve in the shield. If you look inside the curve or crescent, there you will find a wise old owl. Of course the more he heard the less he spoke. If his bill is on the bottom of a stack, his voice would be the softest!

THE OWL

Thinking about the owl lead me to something else. The owl is special because it can turn its head around 360 degrees. I think that I have stated this several times.

ADMIT AND SUBMIT

In my belief system, I believe that when a person is wrong that they should admit the error to themselves. I believe that a person should make a mental note to themselves that they were wrong. Some people might see this as a negative attack upon one's own ego, but I look at it as a positive reinforcement of the participation in the mental growth process. I see it as a well done self pat on the back. If you can't reward yourself for a job well done, then who can? If you find that you were wrong about something of which you had a conversation with someone else about, you should go and admit to the other person that you were wrong. So in this deed, you have admitted your error to yourself and the other person. That is the admit part. That is the easy part. In the next part called to " submit ", you are going to confront the nasty dark side of your ego. Your ego tries to keep the " image " of the self. Your ego says that you are who you are " today ". That state of today could last for years. This is often referred to when someone states that you can't teach a old dog new tricks. Look at the statement. The statement says: " you can't teach a old dog new tricks ". The key to this statement is the term " you "! The you that is being referred to is someone other than the dog. To put this another way, the statement is not saying that the dog can't learn a new trick, but what is being implied is that the dogs ego, or self identity is so embedded in the ego of the dog that it would take a great deal of effort to change the dogs learned behavior. In this case we are talking about a dog. Suppose you put the dog in a fenced yard. You place the dogs food outside of the fence. Wait and see what the dog does. The dog might run around the yard looking for an opening in the fence, jump the fence, dig under the fence, or keep running into the fence until the fence gives way. This is an example of the dog being motivated by external stimuli to become creative to achieve the goal of getting the prize of food. The same can be done with the human ego. Many books have been written about how to bring certain types of situations into being. Really, it just comes down to the stating of " I want ". This using the " I want " part of the ego is very powerful. If you use the " I want " power of the ego to obtain something of ease, the odds of your success are great. When I say something of ease, I mean something that is done in everyday life. Think of wanting to wash your hands at least once a day. What you do is connect the washing of your hands to a task that you already do if you can. How about when you go into the bathroom before you leave you wash your hands. For a while you just keep forgetting. Sometimes you ask yourself " did I wash my hands? " So now you might decide that you need a crutch. You decide to put a sign over the inside of the upper door sill that says: " wash hands ". Sometimes you might need the sign, and sometimes you might not. Then the next thing you know is that you don't need the sign. This pattern goes on for years. Suddenly the cost of water rises. Now you look at this constant washing of your hands as wasting money. Now you have to break the habit. You take down the sign over the door sill if you have not already done that. Now you want to put a sign up over the sink. The sign reads " think before washing hands ". You notice something strange. You notice that you often are reading the sign " as " you are washing your hands. Your sign is not working. You make a sign to place upon a string that hangs from the upper door sill. You want to have to move the sign which breaks the normal pattern that you have. You write on both sides of the sign. Your message needs to be positive. Your message needs to be coded to the ego. You message should invoke the flames of desire in the ego. The ego should create images of you have made this change. You need something that explains to the ego how great it and you will be. Your new sign might read: " You are a great person. You don't waste water which helps the planet and your fellow man. You are a great person! " See, I bet you feel something just reading this. This is one way that humans can project themselves into the future. You could call it using your will " to become ". Remember that this is using or activating the easy positive part of the ego. The harder the goal is to achieve, the more the ego needs to be manipulated. At a certain point there comes something that is called to lock. If the task is great, that means that the task will have an great impact upon the ego, the one may have to lock the ego. This is when the self, of whom is trying to change, and the ego come into conflict. The ego acts as the self written in stone. The ego needs to be reasoned with constantly. This reasoning must take place because the ego becomes aware of " it being changed ". That attempted changing of the ego is what causes " your mind to play trick on you "! I have written about an experiment that was done on the Candid Camera television show. The ego has many ways to " revolt " against you trying to change it which could be called " to have a bad day ". Here is one example of you having a bad day. You decide that you are going to change your behavior in reference to one thing. This change goes against the image of the self that the ego has. The ego acts like a computer in this case. The ego feels that a virus has gotten into the main program of the self. Suppose the task at hand is something like reading The Bible. Now the question is why are you reading The Bible? If you're reading The Bible for ego boosting reasons, it might not be so painful to the ego. Suppose your friends suddenly start reading The Bible and they discuss it all the time. Suppose they are just free with their new activity. Everywhere the group goes they someone brings the subject up. Suddenly you feel that you are a outcast. It is a feeling that is in your mind, but on a certain level it is true. At first you might wait for pauses in the convocation to bring up a new subject. That might even work for a while. Without preplanning, members of the group might start bringing your topics back into the subject of The Bible. That is not hard to do. In fact, it is and unspoken part of the Christian training. I guess I need to give an example here. Suppose you say that you saw a brown dog with black spots. Someone in the group responds about the wonders of Gods creations. You note that the clouds appear as if it is going to rain. Someone responds that it is wonderful how God brings the waters to the plants below. Soon you are going to have to make a choice. Here are some of the choices: 1) be quiet when the subject of God comes up, 2) keep on changing the subject, or 3) start talking about the God subject also. Idea number three sounds great. Besides, the more wrong things that you say, the more attention that you will get. At one point your injection of questionable concepts may be tolerable. That depends how seriously the members of the group are taking The Bible subject. The group could have an open type of feeling towards the subject. I guess I have to give an example of this. Let's talk ice cream. Get say five people together that their favorite flavors are different. Now let the objective of the convocation be why their flavor is the best. Right now we have a problem with our objective statement. The problem is knowledge. First we get fifty people to take part in our experiment. Of each of the fifty people, each on has a favorite flavor in our five control flavors. So now we get fifty people to try the five flavors. We have them list and rate their like of the flavor. The list goes from liked the best to the worst. We want them to rate the flavors from on to ten. Again, here is where we can help " skew " the test results. First, we want to find five flavors that each person likes that is different. Second, we want to find five different flavors that each person just hates. Now all we have to find are the three flavors in between. Again we can " skew " the results by asking which flavor would be the flavor of last resort on a hot day. What flavor would you last choose to eat on a hot day if it was free and all that was available before declining to all of it. We will call this the middle flavor. Really the best, middle, and worst flavors are our concern. Now bring the chosen group of people together to eat ice cream. Now we have them rate the ice cream. We already have an idea of what they are going to chose. At this point, everyone's ego should be neutral. We have learned ways to accept that people are different. Without saying it, we might think that if the other person does not our favorite flavor, then there would be more for us. What a great friend! But now we want to bring the ego into play. Let's have everyone write down what they think is so great about their favorite flavor. Ask them to expound on how the flavor makes them feel. Ask each person as to what type of person might like that flavor. Ask about comments towards the middle flavor. Now here it comes. Ask each person how they fell about their worst picked flavor. Ask each person as to what type of person might like that flavor. Alright, wait a day or so and then bring the five people together to eat ice cream. Place several bowls of ice cream on the table. I guess you need an idea of how many. We want to " skew " our results again. No, we really want to " skew " our results. We started out with five flavors. Now we want to increase the number of flavors. You can go all the way up to 32 or more flavors because all we are going to do is simmer them down using the art of statistics. Say we put five of each person's favorite, middle, and worst flavors on the table. Now we need five of the least liked and second least liked flavors on the table. We don't have anyone write their name upon their comments about the ice cream. As a matter of fact, we type up each person's response. We give a positive response to a person that hated that flavor. As the group eats ice cream, we have them read what someone wrote about the type of person that would like that flavor. No, we need to protect our " **skew** ". We need to have a least two people in the group whose middle ice cream is someone else's worst. Now have them read the results on someone else's choice. After they have read them out loud, we are going to " **skew** " our test again. Have each person read what was said on the result paper given to them about the middle flavor. This is giving time for emotions to build up in the mind. Now have the group have an open conversation about all of the ice cream and wait for the defense of flavors to begin. Where was I? I was talking about the open feeling of a group. The point that I was trying to make was that the stronger that the person feels towards a subject, the more intense that there response to sensitivity will be. I am saying that if the conversation is about a book that has no meaning or reference to the reader, the more open that person will be to foreign ideas. As the group advances in their concepts about The Bible, the more intense the conversations may become. There could come a point where different members of the group may decide not to talk to the ignorant individual at all about the subject. The group may slowly reject the unread one. You might have someone in the group whom expresses a feeling of understanding for the unread person. The sympathizer might even get chastised for being sympathetic to the unlearned person. You might find members of the group saying to the sympathizer things that they are really saying to the unread person. The real cause of the tension is that the unread person is talking about what they don't know about. So what is the big deal? The unread person my introduce concepts into the convocation that seem to require an answer of which the other members are not so sure about. This causes the group members egos to go from a " we are trying to learn " mode to a self blame for not knowing mode. Who wants to be taken into a mode of self blame. It's bad enough that you know that you don't know, but now you are being confronted with the little that you do know mixed with questions and concepts that you can't even begin to answer. Let me put it another way.

BIBLE FRONTER

He is this person playing the fool by saying things that they don't know if they even believe, and they have you wondering about their foolishness of which you feel that you should know is foolishness. You don't know if some of the stuff is foolish or not because you don't clearly understand what you say that you are **believing** in. Now because that person has decided to open their mouth with that foolishness, they have you feeling like " The Fool "! Shut up, that's why the group won't talk to you. Then they enforce their decision using the reason that you could have been reading but you willfully decided not to. The group moves on! The last thing that the unread person needs to know is who they are. They are what is called a " Bible Fronter "! What the average unread Bible Fronter does not know is that they are not alone. There are also people whom go to church every Sunday only to repeat what was said as if it was a concept that they had brought forth from The Bible. Why not appease them? Ask them something simple: " And what does that mean? " Don't wary I'll wait! Yah right!

THE OWLS ADMIT

See, even I did it. At the end of what I just wrote, I had forgotten why I was writing it. When I was writing " Why not appease them ", I had asked myself why was I writing this? My ego is coming up with all kinds of stuff. This is what I call " The Mind Eraser ". The mind eraser is like the Candid Camera example that I gave. Instead of me saying that I was wrong about the owl turning their neck 360 degrees, my ego would rather forget that I was talking about that and move on. Now here is where my ego fights back. My current research now states that a owl can turn their neck 270 degrees. Besides, why should the neck turn 360 degrees. Does the owl have near or greater than 180 degrees of vision with its head still? Well then! Divide 180 degrees in half. That will give you 90 degrees of vision of center of its face. Add the 90 degrees to the 270 degrees, and you have 360 degrees of vision.

THE OWL TOPIC

When I began to think about the owl, I realized that they were carnivores. I began to list all the carnivores that I could. When I got to the snake, I remembered that I had heard some special things about them. I think in most cases, snakes swallow their food whole. I recall it being said that they could dislocate their jaws to fit their food in their mouth. I thought that the snake has to have extremely toxic stomach juices to deal with animals swallowed whole. I then related the strangeness of the snake to The Garden of Eden. I thought to myself " of all of the animals "? As I began to think more on the subject, I thought about dog bites. You often hear about dogs biting someone, but rarely is it said that a dog has eaten someone. It does make sense because as I understand it, once a dog has tasted human blood it has to be " put to sleep ". That makes sense if the tasting of human blood awakens that desire in dogs. I recall thinking that humans may often deal with creatures and situations that they don't fully understand. In thinking about situations that I didn't fully understand, I thought of my question of slavery in America. I just was not happy about my recall of the situation. I recently saw the first episode of " The African Americans: Many Rivers To Cross ". The show was based on the book of the same name by Henry Louis Gates, Jr. and Donald Yacovone. The introduction on page X to Xi reads: " The African Americans: Many Rivers to Cross is a companion book to the six-part, six-hour PBS series of the same title, airing for the first time on national, prime-time broad-cast in the fall of 2013. This book is the basis of the series and presents in much greater detail the 500-year history of the African American people since the black Spanish conquistador, Juan Garrido, accompanied Ponce de Leon on his expedition into what is now the state of Florida. It is entirely fitting that the publication of this book and the airing of the television series coincide with this very important 500th anniversary of the presence of persons of African descent in what is today the continental United States. " The opening scene of how the slaves we acquired from Africa was somewhat unsettling. I just was not sure if this is what I had been told many years ago. With that, it was back to study land. It has been over 30 years and now I am returning to the movie " Roots ".

ROOTS REVISITED

Now I am on the quest to revisit the movie Roots. I found the series at a local store and brought it. I just could not wait to see how the slaves were gotten from Africa. I will talk about this subject another time because it will take me somewhat off of the theme that I am trying to complete here. On one hand it does take me away from what I am trying to do in this document. On the other hand, this bit of information is part of what I am leading to.

FRANK M. CONAWAY, JR.

THE WORLD RECORDS

At this time I feel that I need to clear something up. There seems to be two records of world history. On one hand, there are ancient writings and buildings that point to predating the timeline of Adam < Adam Kadmon > of The Bible; while on the other hand, there is a record of time given in The Bible from the creation of Adam < Adam Kadmon >. The answer seems to be very simple. There appears to be a huge amount of time not recorded from the end of the creation of nature in The Bible to the creation of the biblical Adam < Adam Kadmon >. You see, it was just as easy as that!

KUNDALINI THIS TEXT

In this text I want to end the major story about the topic of Kundalini. With saying that, there are some things that need to be recorded.

MY UNKNOWN KUNDALINI STUDY SEQUENCE

I came across the subject of kundalini in a roundabout way. I was on the path of bible study. I had read The Bible from cover to cover. My first comment about reading The Bible would be that " no one explained it to me like that "! I recall being more confused after reading The Bible for myself than I was before I had read it. I can put it like this, " there was a very serious nature being projected from the book that I was not aware of "! I felt that " I " needed some answers. My awareness had nothing to do with what anybody else felt about that book. I had read it for myself, and therefore " I " had my own opinion. So be it! I started my quest with two things. First, The Bible spoke of obelisks. I did not know what they were nor what they were used for. Second, The Bible made a statement and asked a question at Revelation 13:18. The only clue I had was the one given in the text. I was able to get some sort of start with searching the meaning of the term obelisk. I went along that path while keeping watch for clues to Revelation 13:18. A short time later, I saw a sign in the window of a store. I thought it was some type of African space motherland type of place. I just had never been confronted with anything like that. The store was a great metaphysical resource. I began to learn about metaphysics. I was looking at video lectures of a great number of subjects. Every once in a while one of the lecturers would touch upon things in The Bible. The lecturer might explain the biblical example and it's metaphysical undertones. I then stumbled upon the mother lode. There was something called kundalini that was causing a **frenzy**. It seemed as if every week or so someone had something to say about the kundalini subject. This went on for a few years. The kundalini subject was hot. All kinds of things were being said on the subject. The scientific approach towards the kundalini subject had been covered and covered, and covered again. It seemed as if everyone knew of the kundalini subject, in theory that is! I will put it like this, it is like all of that big foot stuff. I think humans know more about the " big feets " than it knows about its self. I think the only thing that humans don't know about foot is where is it! I suspected the same to be true about kundalini. It was as if a person could be an instant expert on the subject by haven read the most from some secret source I should add. I don't recall anyone saying that on such a such day that they were going to attempt opening the kundalini.

OPEN KUNDALINI AT YOUR OWN RISK

Often the subject of opening the kundalini was talked about with great calmness. Sure, it was like that old walk in the park. Yah right, my research had stated on several occasions that opening the kundalini was very dangerous. The danger was not described in terms of needing a **band aid,** but it being the end of your story. I guess there is no easy way to say that it was said that a person could die attempting to control the kundalini. This is the point that I want to make right here. I concluded that the kundalini process had two main parts to it. I am not talking about the theory of how the kundalini works. The kundalini works just like the tools of the lion **tamer**. There is a wild lion fresh from Africa sitting in a cage. The lion has not eaten in a week. There is a stool in the middle of the cage. Your objective is to make the lion stand on the stool and raise one paw. You go into the cage and yell commands in English at the African lion as if it understands English. The lion becomes confused at your attitude towards it. The lion makes that silly face while trying to **access** the situation. In your lack of patient ions, you crack your whip and fire a cap from your pistol. I really think that you and the lion have a great understanding at this point. This seems to be what is mostly unsaid about kundalini. Kundalini is sometimes described as this great energy of the human body. This energy is not just the raw energy needed to live daily, but also includes the energy to drive human emotions. The kundalini is described as having the raw energy of the human life force and the energy needed to achieve all emotions. I am not talking about one emotion at a time, I am talking about all of the energy of a humans life time and more. When I say more, the kundalini is described as being some sort of free energy type of device. In other words, the kundalini is said to be able to produce its own energy. It is thought of as being like our Sun. Our Sun gives off its energy in a controlled rate, but it could be off balanced whereas it begins to overheat. The concepts of implosion or explosion are not beyond reach. In the first step, the kundalini is set loose. The kundalini is often referred to as a coil. It is called a coil because its energy is thought of as being compressed within it. The kundalini coil could be thought of just as that. Once the band of control is taken off of the kundalini coil, the contained energy can go in several directions. You could even think of riding a very wild bull, but not being able to get off of it. You have to ride the bull until it becomes **tame**. That is the second part of waking the kundalini.

ENTER PARLAMENT FUNKADELIC

Many strange things were taking place around the kundalini subject. It seems as if the subject had been slowly introduced into people's sub consciences. A musical group called Earth, Wind, and Fire had sung about The Serpentine Fire. It appears that this was another name for the kundalini force. Notice how the group's name deals with elements of nature. This is an example of the metaphysics cross over. Earth, Wind, and Fire began to have strange album covers. The artwork could be said to cross over into the mystic metaphysical **arena**. Let's talk about a few of the Earth, Wind, and Fire covers for a minute. Look at The Greatest Hits cover. Do you see the symbols of which some are associated with religions? Do you see the pyramid and Egyptian type wings, eye, and solar disc? Do you see the Egyptian type bird on the Best of Earth, Wind, and Fire volume 1 cover? Do you see the Egyptian pyramid and temple scene on the All N All cover? Do you see three pyramids on the Spirit cover? Is the term " spirit " meant to be an emotion, or a thing as in an entity? Is it far to ask " what's that all about "? Can a message be made any more clear than that? What about Parliament Funkadelic, what's that all about?

Parliament's " Mothership Connection " lyrics say: " Well, all right star child – Citizens of the universe, recording angels - We have returned to claim the pyramids ". Moving on we get to " House Music " and " Jacking Your Body ". The House Music face book page says: " Not everyone understands house music, it's a spiritual thing, a body thing, a soul thing. " There

seems to be a message as they say in the music.

WHO IS THE MASTER

I wrote this heading because it really asks what I feel. It is almost like what happened to Bruce Leroy in the movie The Last Dragon. I wrote Dr. Edward Bruce Bynum, Ph.D. a little while ago. He was nice enough to answer my letter. I think that he has a wonderful book " DARK LIGHT CONSCIOUSNESS – MELANIN, SERPENT POWER, AND THE LUMINOUS MATRIX OF REALITY " ISBN # 978-159477472-0. There is a comment on the rear cover by Teri Degler author of The Divine Feminine Fire and The Fiery Muse. She says: " In this fascinating book, Edward Bynum throws down a gauntlet to science that may very well result in the most revolutionary research ever done on consciousness. " I point to the fact that she refers to this book as being a research document.

ENTER THE QUESTION OF KUNDALINI

There is no question as to if Dr. Bynum has done an excellent job in sharing his extensive research. When I was studying on the kundalini many years ago, the metaphysical masters linked together the topics of physics, neuroscience, biochemistry, holograms, melanin, and more to the kundalini subject. We shall now enter the gray area.

HOW TO SAFELY AWAKEN KUNDALINI

I need to record what is said on the rear cover of Dr. Bynum's book " DARK LIGHT CONSCIOUSNESS – MELANIN, SERPENT POWER, AND THE LUMINOUS MATRIX OF REALITY " ISBN # 978-159477472-0. " Within each of us lies the potential to activate a personal connection to the super conscious. Called "Ureaus" in ancient Egyptian texts and "Kundalini" in ancient Hindu yoga traditions, our innate serpent power of spiritual transcendence inhabits the base of the spine in its dormant state. When awakened, it unfurls along the spinal column to the brain, connecting individual consciousness to the consciousness of the universe enfolded within the dark matter of space. At the root of creativity and spiritual genius across innumerable cultures and civilizations, this intelligent force reveals portals that enfold time, space, and the luminous matrix of reality itself.

Combining physics, neuroscience, and biochemistry with ancient traditions from Africa and India, Edward Bruce Bynum, Ph.D., explores the ancient Egyptian science of the Ureaus and reveals how it is intimately connected to dark matter and to melanin, a light-sensitive, energy-conducting substance found in the brain, nervous system, and organs of all higher life-forms. He explains how the dark light of melanin serves as the biochemical infrastructure for the subtle energy body, just as dark matter, together with gravity, holds the galaxies and constellations together. With illustrated instructions, ' he shows how to safely awaken ' and stabilize the spiritual energy of the Ureaus through meditation practices, breathing exercises, and yoga postures as well as how to prepare the subtle body for transdimensional soul travel.

By embracing the dark light of the shining serpent within, we overcome our collective fear of the vast living darkness without. By embracing the dark, we transcend reality to the dimension of light. " In the given comments above, it is the " he shows how to safely awaken " part that I have question with.

JUMP BACK

This is called the " jump back " because while looking for something I had written in this document, I read this again. In reading it again, and not the second time; well let me explain it to you like this. Come on and play along. If you can find a track of Marshal Jefferson explaining " What Is House " play it in a loop. I lost the place where I was. It was some comment about light from Dr. Bruce Bynum's book. I was looking for the term " light " in this document. The track of Marshal Jefferson explaining " What Is House " was playing in a loop. I then read the comment listed from above as noted from the rear cover of Dr. Bynum's book " DARK LIGHT CONSCIOUSNESS – MELANIN, SERPENT POWER, AND THE LUMINOUS MATRIX OF

REALITY " ISBN # 978-159477472-0. It states: " By embracing the dark light of the shining serpent within, we overcome our collective fear of the vast living darkness without. By embracing the dark, we transcend reality to the dimension of light. " I said to myself what I had said which caused me to buy the book in the first place – ' Say What? '" I need to cipher this step by step < oh, I was looking for what I had written about **Einstein** >: By embracing the dark light < what is dark light? Dark light is dim if visible. Ultra violet rays are sometimes called " dark light " because they are ' beyond ' the human range of vision – see the movie Predator >, By embracing the dark light of the shining serpent within < there is no shining serpent within without the charging and activating principles being applied to the serpent. The serpent is a cord or string so to speak. Without the finger to pluck it, the string only has mathematical potential of a vibratory note. Without the motion of the finger or THE WORD, the string is just a string. The string just sits there and stiffens until it makes its final sound of " snap ". Think of the string as sitting in front of a microphone called the " cosmic record ". The microphone is on listening for a harmonic tone wave or snake. Think of a cosmic cord that extends from one unit say hertz to the maximum string length that reaches across all of creation. I think they now call it the size or greatest diameter of the universe. The shape of the universe came to mind. It would be interesting to see a three dimensional form of what man thinks is creation and where we might be in it. I looked up the shape of an egg. A interesting concept came to view. The concept is that bird eggs are " generally " oval shaped.

HARD VERSES SOFT

At first I thought the strangeness was if a egg was round or oval. I then came across the statement that birds eggs are harder than snake eggs. The I read that some snakes lay eggs, while others don't < What do copperhead snake eggs look like? @ answers.ask.com >. I wonder if there is any other interesting information that will come up upon search? I found that some snakes give live birth: vipers (including rattlesnakes, copperheads, and cottonmouths), boa constrictors, and some North American colubrids such as garter snakes, ribbon snakes, water snakes, earth snakes, and brown snakes.

FRANK M. CONAWAY, JR.

THE THROW OFF: BACK TO THE CIPHERING

JUMP BACK AGAIN

This is called the " jump back " because while looking for something I had written in this document, I read this again. In reading it again, and not the second time; well let me explain it to you like this. Come on and play along. If you can find a track of Marshal Jefferson explaining " What Is House " play it in a loop. I lost the place where I was. It was some comment about light from Dr. Bruce Bynum's book. I was looking for the term " light " in this document. The track of Marshal Jefferson explaining " What Is House " was playing in a loop. I then read the comment listed from above as noted from the rear cover of Dr. Bynum's book " DARK LIGHT CONSCIOUSNESS – MELANIN, SERPENT POWER, AND THE LUMINOUS MATRIX OF REALITY " ISBN # 978-159477472-0. It states: " By embracing the dark light of the shining serpent within, we overcome our collective fear of the vast living darkness without. By embracing the dark, we transcend reality to the dimension of light. " I said to myself what I had said which caused me to buy the book in the first place – ' Say What? '" I need to cipher this step by step < oh, I was looking for what I had written about **Einstein** >: By embracing the dark light < what is dark light? Dark light is dim if visible. Ultra violet rays are sometimes called " dark light " because they are ' beyond ' the human range of vision – see the movie Predator >, By embracing the dark light of the shining serpent within < there is no shining serpent within without the charging and activating principles being applied to the serpent. The serpent is a cord or string so to speak. Without the finger to pluck it, the string only has mathematical potential of a vibratory note. Without the motion of the finger or THE WORD, the string is just a string. The string just sits there and stiffens until it makes its final sound of " snap ". Think of the string as sitting in front of a microphone called the " cosmic record ". The microphone is on listening for a harmonic tone wave or snake. Think of a cosmic cord that extends from one unit say hertz to the maximum string length that reaches across all of creation. I think they now call it the size or greatest diameter of the universe. The shape of the universe came to mind. It would be interesting to see a three dimensional form of what man thinks is creation and where we might be in it. I looked up the shape of an egg. A interesting concept came to view. The concept is that bird eggs are " generally " oval shaped. STOP! I have to look to see if there is an estimated size of the universe < Why is our universe flat? @ answers.com > .

WHAT TYPE OF SET IS THIS

All I want you to do is go to Google search and type in " shape of our universe ". Well, what do you think about that? What a side track!

THE THROW OFF: BACK TO THE CIPHERING

JUMP BACK AGAIN 2

This is called the " jump back " because while looking for something I had written in this document, I read this again. In reading it again, and not the second time; well let me explain it to you like this. Come on and play along. If you can find a track of Marshal Jefferson explaining " What Is House " play it in a loop. I lost the place where I was. It was some comment about light from Dr. Bruce Bynum's book. I was looking for the term " light " in this document. The track of Marshal Jefferson explaining " What Is House " was playing in a loop. I then read the comment listed from above as noted from the rear cover of Dr. Bynum's book " DARK LIGHT CONSCIOUSNESS – MELANIN, SERPENT POWER, AND THE LUMINOUS MATRIX OF REALITY " ISBN # 978-159477472-0. It states: " By embracing the dark light of the shining serpent within, we overcome our collective fear of the vast living darkness without. By embracing the dark, we transcend reality to the dimension of light. " I said to myself what I had said which caused me to buy the book in the first place – ' Say What? '" I need to cipher this step by step < oh, I was looking for what I had written about Einstein >: By embracing the dark light < what is dark light? Dark light is dim if visible. Ultra violet rays are sometimes called " dark light " because they are ' beyond ' the human range of vision – see the movie Predator >, By embracing the dark light of the shining serpent within < there is no shining serpent within without the charging and activating principles being applied to the serpent. The serpent is a cord or string so to speak. Without the finger to pluck it, the string only has mathematical potential of a vibratory note. Without the motion of the finger or THE WORD, the string is just a string. The string just sits there and stiffens until it makes its final sound of " snap ". Think of the string as sitting in front of a microphone called the " cosmic record ". The microphone is on listening for a harmonic tone wave or snake. Think of a cosmic cord that extends from one unit say hertz to the maximum string length that reaches across all of creation. I think they now call it the size or greatest diameter of the universe. The shape of the universe came to mind. It would be interesting to see a three dimensional form of what man thinks is creation and where we might be in it. I looked up the shape of an egg. A interesting concept came to view. The concept is that bird eggs are " generally " oval shaped. STOP! I have to look to see if there is an estimated size of the universe. Alright < here loop > So my point at this point is that there may be many different diameter cords for the universe. When connected together they may create a tone of many cords. This is how many cords could fit within a tone, while even more might not. The cord that we are speaking of over time would naturally collect cosmic dust. The dust adds weight to the cord. Then also over time, the length of the cord stretches. In other words, the cord becomes out of tune with its original tone. I will put my conclusion on this statement under " THE SAME OLD CORD ".

IS IT THE SAME

The question I have here is the " safe " awakening of the kundalini the same as the traditional exercise? I can see how a person could gather so much data that they could appear as being an expert on the subject. I guess in being honest, Dr. Bynum's work is outstanding. In a strange way, a piece of work like this could be a **hindrance**. The book seems to be so well done that there appears as if there is no research left to do. It just seems as if Dr. Bynum has all of the answers. His work is on the order of being able to measure if a person has done the kundalini exercise or not. I guess for me, his work is " a " proof as to that I know what I am talking about!

DARK LIGHT AND THE BIBLE

I guess in a way, this text is useful to me because I can easily point to what I am talking about. Now that I have said that, the situation seems kind of funny. Watch this. If we go to the index of the book and look for bible, we find the following pages listed: " 11, 76, 80, 90, 251, and 296 ". I would like to also note that the word bible is spelled with a capital " B "! When we look for Jesus, we find no listing. There is a listing for: " Judas, Gospel of ". I am starting to think that it is funny. I will talk about this next. If we go to page 348 of the index, we find that the term " Christ " is listed on pages: " 55, 76, 140, 251, 293, 311, and 320 ".

KUNDALINI SEXUAL TANTRA

Sometimes a subject is what it is or what it is made of. This is the case for Kundalini Sexual Tantra. That was the main topic title. This is like all of the knowledge related to this topic. I found that some people would find the concepts **bizarre** to the point that they would feel as if I had made the concept up. I had first heard about the concept in the early 1970's. The theory was put forth in the movie " Ilsa: She Wolf of the S. S. ". The theory really became active when the concept of the kundalini came into the picture. There was talk of the need to build one's vital reserve for the kundalini process. No reason was given that I can remember. The concept had to do with building " chi ". I recall reading about a theory where the " chi " was to be converted into " chang ". This chi and chang relationship was a part of Kundalini Sexual Tantra. You could think of it as the concept being thought of but being used passively. The aggressive side of Kundalini Sexual Tantra was dealing with actively cultivating one's chi. This was done by things that could be done. The active side of Kundalini Sexual Tantra is what is self named as " The One Thousand Strokes of the Chinaba < chi - na – ba > **techniques**. It is nice to see the Kama Sutra is said to be mentioned on page 151. Tantra is not listed in the index. On page 150 Dr. Bynum writes: " The bodily energies tend to be devalued or suppressed in traditional psychospiritual disciplines. This body-negative bias is not embraced here. Many of the sexual and strange genitourinary practices found in classic yogic disciplines are either simply omitted or become the source of repulsion for devotees and teachers in the modern world. The classic Hatha Yoga Pradipka of Swami Svatmarama describes and advocates the practices of Amaroli, Vajroli, and Sahajoli as methods of sublimating and redirecting the sexual fluids from their downward course out into the world of brief spasm of pleasure that leaves the organism feeling depleted. Instead there is the practice of re-absorpon by the body, spinal line, and ultimately the brain. Beyond these methods being quite awkward and difficult, it is the attitude of negativity toward sexuality and bodily functions that is so disturbing among some of these writers and practitioners. Sexuality and the subtle hormonal fluids and essences associated with the body are natural resources to be harnessed and directed. This includes the greatly misunderstood group and tantric practices so repugnant to the Aryan and Semitic intuitions that underlie much of the religious perception of sexuality found in Christianity, Islam, and large areas of Hinduism. These practices incorporate group and ritualistic yoni and lingam or phallic worship and sexual union as well as the tamer Maithuna Sadhana of the couple. These are the roots of the sacred energetic practices found in the Kama Sutra. " There is so much that I could say about this, but right now the concept of the book really appears to break away or trim down on the given ancient way of dealing with the kundalini. I think that the questioning of several steps of the handed down tradition is a valid concept. On the other hand, this is a prime reason why the ancients would keep this type of knowledge hidden. In other words, how is it that a person that has not done the sequence is conceptualizing changing a system that may be thousands of years old.

WHO ARE YOU

The teachings are becoming very strange now. The ancients had also warned of them whom would come and try to change the traditions. The concepts that are being considered for change have real meanings as to why the techniques are included. At this point, it is only fair to call opening the kundalini a ritual. In this case, you must realize how much tradition Dr. Bynum is going against. This type of thinking is often associated with what is called the western thought pattern. I had wanted to comment on " THE ROLE OF DIAPHRAGMATIC BREATHING AND THE FIRST AND TENTH CRANIAL NERVES " from pages 225 to 226. I really had something to say about " THE TONGUE ON THE UPPER PALATE " on pages 226 to 227. What was not said in these two sections made me feel funny about this work.

MASKED PROBLEMS

At this point I have a few problems with Dr. Bynum's book " DARK LIGHT CONSCIOUSNESS – MELANIN, SERPENT POWER, AND THE LUMINOUS MATRIX OF REALITY " ISBN # 978-159477472-0. There seems to be two sides to the book. The first side deals with the research that has been done. If that was half of the grade, this document would be half way home. This is to say that the research document " DARK LIGHT CONSCIOUSNESS – MELANIN, SERPENT POWER, AND THE LUMINOUS MATRIX OF REALITY " ISBN # 978-159477472-0 is of the highest order. In a strange way this collection of information is exactly what I did. I found that some of the information over lapped, while some of the information took other paths. The research I was doing became very strange. In some cases people began to write about the " kundalini " subject as if they knew exactly what they knew what they were talking about. The strange part about the kundalini writings was that there was really no way to tell if a person knew if they knew what they were talking about or not! In the eubonic sense that is called to front. This type of fronting is on the second level of fronting. The first level of fronting is to present the research information without saying that the document is " a report upon research ' ONLY '. The second level of fronting becomes very confusing. The researcher presents their research into the kundalini subject with " the addition of conclusions without saying that the conclusions that are being presenting are based on ' SWAG '". When I was in high school I was taught about a certain way to approach a scientific method of solving a problem. Think of a multiple choice question with several given answers. The researcher gathers all of the information that they can. After all of the available information is gathered, the answers that are ruled out are taken off of the list. It does not matter how many possible answers there are in the opening statement, the key is the rule out any answers that appear false. In middle school I learned about this type of approach. I was taught that this way of approaching a problem was called " to use the scientific method ". This type of way of thought has rules to it. One rule is that the way that the question is being asked is of such a manner that the opening statement prejudices the possible answers. This type of error can cause the researcher a certain type of problem. The researcher can become " stuck " in their research because what is not included in their list of options " of answers.

DUMMY

What else can I call this type of researcher. In a strange way, the research steals their own reward away from themselves. By the researchers work being on the highest level, the researcher should always be given credit for their contribution upon the subject. The researcher disqualifies themselves from being rewarding due to fronting. In most cases a researcher is a part of a sequential order of investigation upon a subject. Let me make this theory clear to you. Let us call the beginning of the investigation into a subject level one. Level one is the awareness of the question of what is that? Levels two to nine are the research results that lead to the answer of the question. The process of the transit of the levels of research from two to nine can lead to many answers that are outside of the original set of possible answers. When one or more of these new possible conclusions are the result of the study of a conclusion, the whole process has to be repeated from the beginning with these new possible conclusions added to the opening statement. I was taught that the beginning approach to the solving of a problem is called the " observation ". This is the second level step of the way or path of investigation into a subject. This is what I was taught about the way of the scientific method of investigation of a subject. The first thing to do is to make a statement about what the subject is that you are going to investigate. In this case, this is where you can tell a lot about the researcher. In many cases you can tell many things about the researcher without being aware of what is behind the facemask of the researcher.

FACEMASK

The question at this point is why would a researcher " taint " their own research conclusions? Why don't you stop here and ask yourself " why would someone do such a thing? There are a few answers to this question. I collected all of the information that I could find on the subject of kundalini. A person could collect all of the available information on a subject that they could find. This takes us to the second level of our " scientific method ". The first thing to do is to make a statement about what the subject is that you are going to investigate. The second level is to state all of the observations about the subject that you can. At this point the researcher has to be mindful of their own sneaky ego. The ego in this case can concluded that the researcher should be rewarded for " the great effort "! This is a clear mistake of the powerful ego. The reward is in the presentation of " pure " evidence " of the observed truths. This is called to see. In many cases to see does not lead to the level of " to know ". In this new age, there is talk of " dark matter ". Dark matter is said to be a " thing " or " substance " that acts one way when it is not being observed and another way when it is being investigated ".

SOMETHING ELSE IS GOING ON

This is where research becomes a task. The researcher is collection pure data. To collect pure data is to record that only what is seen. At certain point this becomes very hard to do. In many cases this is where words of wisdom come into play. The way that the wisdom is presented might not even be related to the subject on face value.

THE TRUMPSTER'S WISDOM

Many years ago I saw Donald Trump being interviewed on television. Mr. Trump was asked if he " were " going to give someone so advice about how to approach life from a financial perspective, what advice would he give. I could tell that the interview had suddenly become of an uncomfortable level. I have to say what many people say about Mr. Trump. To several people, Mr. Trump is referred to as THE TRUMPSTER. This name is a reflection of how it is perceived that Mr. Trump moves about play at the game of life. In some cases one can watch what is perceived as Mr. Trump " taking a loss ". In many cases, many people become happy to see Mr. Trump " FAIL ". I must say that this type of person is off the most hated type of human on the planet. < By the way, this is what was said. Look at all the people you know. If you do what they do as work, most likely you will end up with the same results as they have. If you don't want those results, you might as well try something else! >

THE HATERS

These type of people are so great that they have been awarded their own category of recognition. They are called " THE HATERS "! I don't even want to talk about them because they are so so very sorry. Don't wary THE HATERS are not alone. THE HATERS have a related group of friends called " THE BLOCKERS ". The haters hate, while the blockers block. What you have to understand is the nature of these peoples ego. The hater might hate you for doing what they won't do. They might be in position long before you, but they won't even think about doing what has to be done. Why you might ask? Suppose if I told you that you are going to have to suffer the worst type of punishment for trying to do what's right! Are you surprised?

See how one topic can lead to many different subjects. I am just pointing out how this happens and not saying that this type of deviation is meaningless. This shift of subject is needed because you need to add these **possibilities** because they should be included in your scientific method. At this point I just wondered what the haters are going to say about this that I am writing? In a way it's funny because the haters are going to formulate opinions about what I am writing without trying to be seen in the light of why I am writing this about them!

YOGIST MASTER

Enter the thought of " THE YOGIST MASTER ". As long as the very raggedy mouth is speaking, it is all good. Watch this! The haters can hate all they want to. Comedian Cat Williams made a comment about needing more haters! Come on haters, haters come on! Now watch this.

THE HATERS NIGHTMARE

How do you deal with the hater? You don't! How do you acknowledge the hater? You don't. Their object is to play mind games on you. Their worst result is to have you play mind games with them! If they want to burn up their life-force nay saying you, let them. If what you are doing is called " minding your own business " and they become irritated, all they are doing is expressing their negative side in its purest form.

FLASHLIGHT YOUR HATER

You have to turn the lights on. Turn your attention to the motions of the haters. The haters are like cock roaches. When the lights are off, these cock roaches get very involved in your business. In many cases they have opinions about what someone else should be doing.

HATER BE GONE

I can give you an example of serious hate. One day I saw a man get out of his car and go into the store. The car was a very serious expensive sports car. I guess my mind was not ready for what I was about to see. The man got out of his space ship type sports car. He began to walk to the store when my vision was broken by conflicting information. Here is this very expensive car, and there is it's raggedy muffin driver. His tennis shoes were the oldest dirtiest worn-out funky shoes that I can really say that I had ever seen anyone that owns a car wearing. I mean if you took them to the Good Will, the counter attendant would ask what do you want to be done with the shoe like objects. No really, these are the type of shoes that you wash and that friendly smell jumps right out as you begin to put them on. Enough about the shoes, but I could go on about the nasty laces. Look at his jeans. Raggedy with frizzes and holes can't even describe them. I guess I have to say that this happened long before ragged jeans became vogue. Ah, I know the origin of this stupid money making fashion trick. Here is the last part of the vision. The tee shirt had to have been worn several times. Now that I think of it, I think this type of behavior is often show on television. I have been missing the joke because it is outside of " my " personal culture. Maybe some people have their after work cloths that they put in a special place. When I say a special place, I am talking about in a corner or under the bed. The attire might go months or years without being washed. In a way it is not nasty. Think of a favorite spot that you have in your bed. Alright, we have now defined your spot. Someone one day does you a favor and makes up your bed. They even change your favorite cartoon character sheets. Oh by the way, because the sheets were torn they threw the sheets away. Good thing for you that it was trash day. That is the tee shirt that I am talking about. As a note, I don't know if I am going to talk about it here, but getting rid of that shirt is part of the yogis detachment. You see how by noting that I have to add more so that you don't get the wrong ideas.

FOR YOU AND THE HATERS

Sure it is great to have a lot of material things. I often think of what I am going to do with all of the books that I had to " consume " to make it to this point. They are like drained batteries. What good are they to me? Really the knowledge of the books are for you and the haters. Remember how I was talking about the haters? On one hand the knowledge of these books is for you whom are on the path. I don't know what path you are on. Maybe these books will be of no use to you, but they might just be helpful in shutting the haters down. When the hater begins to **criticize** you, don't get mad. Share the love. Show them the images of the books that they are unaware of. As for me, my answer is: " I wasn't talking to you, I was just saying; _ A _ _ _ < or is that " I " >! "

COUNTER EGO

Watch what happens to " their ego "! This is a part of what is called " the secrete techniques' of mind boxing ". I am aware that I am so far off, and I know why. I am getting ready to tell you that the hater in me jumped out. I began to think of all the reasons why I would not be dressed like that while driving that car. Then my " counter ego " checked my ego. I have never heard this term before, nor had I a reason to name what it is. I have to give it a name in order to convey the idea to you. My counter ego said to my ego: " maybe that's why you don't have a car like that. Yeh, see; you are ready to allow the car to define how you act! " I will not that I didn't like the yogis type answer. So where are we? We are dealing with the scientific method. A person could collect all of the available information on a subject that they could find. This takes us to the second level of our " scientific method ". The first thing to do is to make a statement about what the subject is that you are going to investigate. The second level is to state all of the observations about the subject that you can. At this point the researcher has to be mindful of their own sneaky ego. I have already told you something about the ego in reference to scientific investigation. I really don't want to go to the next level, but how can I go past it if I know how to go through it.

EGO DUMMY

I had been doing study on how The Great Pyramid of/at Giza was built. That was the question of the day. Looking back on the situation, that was about the dumbest question of all times. I have heard it said that the only dumb question is the question that is not asked. Alright,

I will agree with that. So what is the first of the least intelligent questions that can be asked? Really! How did they get those stones all the way up there? Really! How did they cut those stones so accurately? See, this is what I have been wanting to tell you about. I didn't know why I wanted to detail this, but I know now.

KEY: SPIRITUAL KUNDALINI DANGER

That's why! The reason is because of " SPIRITUAL KUNDALINI DANGER "! I have a title in mind, but I need to check myself before I open my mouth. No, I can check myself while still making this statement. The concept of a Grand Turkey Wizard came to mind. In most cases there were two great warnings dealing with the kundalini subject. The first warning had to do with an external challenge as one approaches the study of the kundalini. The second warning had to do with an internal challenge that one faces once the internal process is begun. That is the point of no return. I need to backup about the first statement. It seems that there is a penalty for even approaching the kundalini concept. In a way I would say that it is like playing Church. From the spiritual sense, once a person is made aware of the spiritual path, the " dark matter " of this world changes how it deals with you! I was getting around to the two ways that I have seen the knowledge of the kundalini written about. One way I have seen the kundalini talked about was from a purely physical scientific method of dealing with it. From what I have read and my opinion, this is extremely dangerous. In one of The Matrix movies Neo is taken down to the control room where everything happens. The statement of not knowing how it all works is made. This is my point of the second and most dangerous part of the kundalini.

SAFELY AWAKEN

On the rear cover of Dr. Bynum's book " DARK LIGHT CONSCIOUSNESS – MELANIN, SERPENT POWER, AND THE LUMINOUS MATRIX OF REALITY " ISBN # 978-159477472-0 it is written: " With illustrated instructions, he shows how to safely awaked and stabilize the spiritual energy of the Ureaus through meditation practices, breathing exercises, and yoga postures as well as how to prepare the subtle body for transdimensional soul travel. " I

wondered what Dr. Bynum had to say about this subject and religion. I found the term " religion
" listed in the index on page 355: " 7 - 8, 246 – 49, 311 and Clear Light experience, 277, 280 ". I
then noticed " Revelation, Book of, 80 ".

IS KUNDALINI UREAUS

On page 7 - 8 of Dr. Bynum's book " DARK LIGHT CONSCIOUSNESS – MELANIN,
SERPENT POWER, AND THE LUMINOUS MATRIX OF REALITY " ISBN # 978-
159477472-0 it is written: " We will make an explicit connection between spiritual practice and
the physical world, particularly our bodies. Specifically when exploring the ' energetic ' aspects
of practice we will show that while air and oxygen are not the subtle energy of prana or ki/chi,
they are intimately related. Similarly the dark reality of neuromelanin is not identical to the
psychospiritual dynamism of kundalini, the Ureaus, but they are intimately related. Harness one
and you influence the other. This over bridge and connection will provide a basis for clinical and
scientific observation in our present-day understanding of spiritual unfoldment. This is crucial
for our age. With so many ' gospels ' and scriptures being discovered, questioned, historically
banished, and then reaccepted into old (e.g., the Gospel of Magdalene, the Gospel of Thomas),
it is important to be guided by a gospel based on scientific replication and own direct experience.
" Later on that page he states: " We are all Homo sapiens sapiens, descendents and permutations
of the ancient ones who arose in Africa and spread their progeny around the Earth. In evolution
we have common origin; in our DNA we share a common heritage. In neurobiology we have a
common neural network upon which our spiritual music has learned to play. Our brains, organ
systems, spinal cords, and our subtle nervous systems bind us each together in an intimate
mysterious way. "

SPIRITUIAL CONFUSION

**I disagree. This is another one of those very advanced statements that appears to
take a stance, but is two faced. The history of The Bible that I read states that there were
two creations of beings that might have " looked " somewhat the same. I make both of**

these statements based upon the person called Cain of The Bible. Cain makes the statement in Genesis 4 that whoever finds him would kill him. Why does he say that? How could Cain be told apart from other human types? I bring this out to say that the " we " that you speak of might not be a group called " us ". What I am Saying is that the song says " When we all get to Heaven! " First of all, who is " we "? Second of all, not all people are trying to go to the same Heaven, or any Heaven as far as that is concerned!

PRESS STOP - INTERUPT AT GENESIS 4:13 KEY

< I have to break in here. I have already done 192 pages of this book. I need to add this. At Genesis 4:13 - 15, Cain states that 1) " today you are driving me from the land, " 2) " AND I WILL BE HIDDEN FROM YOUR PRESENCE ". This is key, very key. You can compare the versions at " biblestudytools.com ". Now if you go to " gotquestions.org/mark-Cain.html ", you find the comment that " Cain's line was terminated by the flood. " So who died in Genesis? Was it Adam? Was it Abel? Was it Cain? Was it two or three of them? Does that change the meaning of what the snake said when it said to Adam that he, Adam shall not surly die? Is that funny, hum? Wow! > On page 248 there is talk about " the Kabbalistic discipline of the Jewish mystical tradition. " " What is crucial here, however, is that through its central texts, the Sefer Yetzirah and Zohar: The Book Of Splendor, a method is elaborated for union with God. " Good for me, I have already read them; so and I have an understanding of what they are talking about. I was going to write " I wonder what's next? " On to page 311 which reads: " The esoteric Christ constantly spoke of the stars that lived within us. " A reference to the source of this statement is given on page 335 under CHAPTER 13. THE GOAL AND THE ATTAINMENT says that the statement number 9 comes from " Kasser, Meyer, and Wurst, The Gospel of Judas. " This is a little interesting because comment number 1 is from the same source. Let's go and check it out. Comment number 1 is found on page 293. " Eventually, there is the appearance of beings and forces. Some of these great Beings of light and intelligence move freely in the dimensions beyond all our conceptualization. Even those curled-up, compacted dimensions reverberating through our current-day multiverse of string theory are only a pale intuition of this. It is the realm of the unspeakable, " the

immortal realm of Barbelo " in the Gnostic an Sethian texts that is even beyond this imperfect world of the creator God in which we find ourselves. I disagree with this concept. I think that this world is just perfect for who " we " are. First we were on the Adamic level of perfection. No, let me change this. I think that this world is just perfect for biblically what it may be. From nbcnews.com on 12/08/ 2013: " Satanists want statue beside Ten Commandments monument at Oklahoma Legislature ".

I added this to show my point. I went to the internet to see what is said about the " biblical threshing floor ". I first went to bible-history.com where there were many examples of the threshing floor in the bible. I noticed that no examples were given of The New Testament. I continued my search on biblegateway.com. 40 examples were given. Two examples were given from The New Testament. This was what I was looking for. A strange thing happened. The threshing floor was the second thing that I was going to talk about on the page I had written. The first topic I was going to write about was what The Bible says about mans mindset. I need not go into it because it is listed as the last entry from " biblical threshing floor ". Here are the last three results given < I don't know what search engine that I used, but blueletterbible.org has several more answers >.

Micah 4:12-But they do not know the thoughts of the LORD; they do not understand his plan, that he has gathered them like sheaves to the **threshing floor**.

Matthew 3:12-His winnowing fork is in his hand, and he will clear his **threshing floor**, gathering his wheat into the barn and burning up the chaff with unquenchable fire."

Luke 3:17-His winnowing fork is in his hand to clear his **threshing floor** and to gather the wheat into his barn, but he will burn up the chaff with unquenchable fire."

What this does is leads The Bible reader to a understanding that everyone of this place called Earth is not going to same place " after this life ".

Exodus 23:13- "Be careful to do everything I told you. "Never mention the **names of** other **god**s or let them be heard on your lips.

Deuteronomy 12:3- Tear down their altars, crush their sacred stones, burn their poles dedicated to the **god**dess Asherah, cut down their idols, and wipe out the **names of** their **god**s from those places. Joshua 23:7- Don't get mixed up with the nations left in your territory. Don't ever mention the **names of** their **god**s or swear an oath to them. Don't ever serve their **god**s or bow down to them.

Psalm 16:4- Those who quickly chase after other **god**s multiply their sorrows. I will not pour out their sacrificial **offerings of** blood or use my lips to speak their **names**.

Hosea 2:17- I won't allow her to say the **names of** other **god**s called Baal. She will never again call out their **names**.

Micah 4:5- All the nations live by the **names of** their **god**s, but we will live by the name **of Yahweh** our **Elohim** forever.

Hebrews 12:23- and to the assembly **of God**'s firstborn children (whose **names** are written in heaven). You have come to a judge (the **God of** all people) and to the spirits **of** people who have **God**'s approval and have gained eternal life.

NAMES OF GOD

While looking up threshing floor on biblegateway.com, I came across the heading " The Names Of God " < look it up >.

AFTER " EARTH " LIFE IS REALLY THE QUESTION

Is there a " after life " is really the question? That is the question on the first level. Once a person comes to grips with that concept, the idea of " more than one place to go " comes into play. Which " after life " place becomes the second question? Now a third problem comes into question, how do you get where you want to go? Once a person decides that THE CHRIST CHRISTIAN HEAVEN is where they want to go, they have to deal with their mindset.

THEY GREVED THE LORD

I would suggest that you go and read what is said about " the threshing floor "

The general mindset of man was spoken of in The Bible during the time of Noah. Let's check with biblegateway.com to see what is said in a word search of Noah. Here are a few of the 56 things that were said.

Genesis 6:13- So God said to **Noah**, "I am going to put an end to all people, for the earth is filled with violence because of them. I am surely going to destroy both them and the earth.

Genesis 9:24- When **Noah** awoke from his wine and found out what his youngest son had done to him,

Matthew 24:37- As it was in the days of **Noah**, so it will be at the coming of the Son of Man.

Matthew 24:38- For in the days before the flood, people were eating and drinking, marrying and giving in marriage, up to the day **Noah** entered the ark;

Luke 17:26- "Just as it was in the days of **Noah**, so also will it be in the days of the Son of Man.

Luke 17:27- People were eating, drinking, marrying and being given in marriage up to the day **Noah** entered the ark. Then the flood came and destroyed them all.

Hebrews 11:7- By faith **Noah**, when warned about things not yet seen, in holy fear built an ark to save his family. By his faith he condemned the world and became heir of the righteousness that is in keeping with faith.

1 Peter 3:20- to those who were disobedient long ago when God waited patiently in the days of **Noah** while the ark was being built. In it only a few people, eight in all, were saved through water,

2 Peter 2:5- if he did not spare the ancient world when he brought the flood on its ungodly people, but protected **Noah**, a preacher of righteousness, and seven others; etc.

In my other writing BAPTIST GNOSTIC CHRISTIAN EUBONIC KUNDALINION SPIRITUAL KI DO HERMENEUTIC METAPHYSICS ISBN #0595206780, I spoke of the brazen serpent. I decided to look up " brazen " on biblegateway and here are the three results that came up.

Proverbs 7:13- She took hold of him and kissed him and with a **brazen** face she said:

Jeremiah 3:3- Therefore the showers have been withheld, and no spring rains have fallen. Yet you have the **brazen** look of a prostitute; you refuse to blush with shame.

Ezekiel 16:30- "'I am filled with fury against you, declares the Sovereign LORD, when you do all these things, acting like a **brazen** prostitute!

WHAT VERSION: NEHUSHTAN

Now I shall look up " brazen serpent " like I started to. No results were found. How could that be? The search is said to be in the New International Version of The Bible. Let me try another version. I changed the search to the New King James Version of The Bible. No match was found. I decided to do a general internet search on Google. The search of " brazen serpent " on Wikipedia **leads** to the term " nehushtan " < Wikipedia >. Moses lifts up the brass snake, curing the Israelites of snakebites. Hezekiah called the snake Nehushtan < The Nehushtan (or Nehustan), in the Hebrew Bible, was a sacred object in the form of a snake of brass upon a pole. The priestly source of the Torah says that Moses used a 'fiery serpent' to cure the Israelites from snakebites. (Numbers 21:4-9) King Hezekiah (reigned 715/716 – 687 BCE) instituted a religious iconoclastic reform and destroyed "the brazen serpent that Moses had made; for unto those days the children of Israel did offer to it; and it was called Nehushtan." (2 Kings 18:4) The tradition of naming it Nehushtan is no older than the time of Hezekiah. In 1508 Michelangelo's image of the Israelites deliverance from the plague of serpents by the creation of the bronze serpent on the ceiling of the Sistine Chapel >.

SNAKE CULTS CIPHER

Snake cults < clue: FMCJR – also the movie Conan < in Canaan = letters: i n c a = Cain > The Barbarian > < YOU REALLY NEED TO LOOK UP SNAKE CULTS. I WILL TELL YOU WHY. I HAVE THIS LITTLE BIBLE THING THAT I ASK MYSELF ABOUT BIBLICIAL THINGS. I ASK MYSELF HOW DOES WHAT I AM THINKING ABOUT RELATE TO THE GARDEN OF EDEN. < JUST TO ADD: ADAM AND EVE WE " CAST " OUT OF THE GARDEN OF EDEN. WHAT ARE THE LETTERS OF EDEN? THE LETTERS ARE: E – D – E – N. THE CONSTANATS ARE D –N. THE VOWELS ARE: E –E, OR TWO E's. E TAKEN TO THE SECOND LEVEL IS WHAT? LET'S COUNT OUR VOWELS BY VOWEL: A – E – I – O – U and sometimes Y. THE FIRST LEVEL OF " E " IS " E ". THE SECOND LEVEL OF " E " IS 2 TIMES 2, WHICH IS AE-IO. THE ANSWER IS " O ". SO NOW WE TAKE THIS REDUCTION

OF THE FOR LETTERS DOWN TO 3 LETTERS. THIS SOUNDS LIKE A
TETRAGRAMATION EXERCISE. SO WE HAVE: D – N – O. WHAT COULD IT
SPELL? >

WHICH FALL OF MAN

    < I WAS GOING TO MAKE YOU WAIT ON IT, BUT WHO HAS TIME FOR
SILLY GAMES; ALTHOUGHT IT WAS GOING TO BE FUNNY. HOW ABOUT I PUT
IT LIKE THIS, WHERE DID CAIN GO AFTER HE WAS KICKED OUT OF THE
PLACE WHERE ADAM AND EVE HAD BEEN KICKED OUT OF EDEN TO? > < SO
ADAM AND EVE WERE KICKED OUT OF PLACE NUMBER ONE TO PLACE
NUMBER TWO. THEN CAIN WAS KICKED OUT OF PLACE NUMBER TWO TO
PLACE NUMBER THREE WHERE HE WAS DON(E) < I am saying done, rather don as
in to reverse don to nod, the land where Cain went. >. < SURPOSE IN THIS CASE THE "
E " AGAIN WAS THE SYMBOL FOR ENERGY. < FROM WIKIPEDIA: THE POUND
OR POUND-MASS IS A UNIT OF MASS USED IN THE IMPERIAL, UNITED STATES
CUSTOMARY AND OTHER SYSTEMS OF MEASUREMENT. A NUMBER OF
DIFFERENT DEFINITIONS HAVE BEEN USED, THE MOST COMMON TODAY
BEING THE INTERNATIONAL AVOIRDUPOIS POUND WHICH IS LEGALLY
DEFINED AS EXACTLY 0.45359237 KILOGRAMS, AND WHICH IS DIVIDED INTO
16 AVOIRDUPOIS OUNCES > SURPOSE IN SOME SORT OF WAY A PERSONS
MASS HAD TO BE EQUAL TO OR LESS THAN THEIR BIRTH WEIGHT CALLED
THE EGYPTIAN " LIGHTER THAN A FEATHER? " < THESE ARE QUESTIONS
THAT OPEN INSIDE OF THOUGHTS. THE QUESTION I HAVE NOW IS IT
POSSIBLE THAT SIN HAS A TYPE OF WEIGHT? I DON'T NEED TO ASK THAT.
NO, SIN IS A THING. SIN IS LIKE A SUNTAN OR A UNIVERSAL BIRTH MARK. I
WOULD SAY A TYPE OF NAVEL, BUT WHO KNOWS WHAT'S GOING ON WITH
CLONING AND SCIENCE THESE DAYS? >

WHAT IS SIN

    From biblestudytools.com, the first listing for the search of " sin " is at Genesis 4:7 of the
NIV Bible which reads: " If you do what is right, will you not be accepted? But if you do not do
what is right, sin is crouching at your door; it desires to have you, but you must master it."

I think that we need to go just a little bit deeper.

GENESIS 4 PROBLEM: MORE SIN

Sin: From Wikipedia, the free encyclopedia: < " WHAT, IS THERE SOME KIND OF LEVEL OF SIN FORCE FIELD AROUND THESE PLACES, OR COULD THEY BE DEMINSIONS. WAIT, I FORGOT ABOUT THE FIRST DIMENSION PRIME, THAT HAS TO BE THE PLACE BEFORE THE ADAMIC STORY TOOK PLACE WHERE KICKED OUT AND DOWN CAIN GOT HIS WIFE FROM. THE PLACE WHERE IF THEY FROM THERE FOUND HIM, THEY WOULD KILL HIM. SO A " MARK " WAS PUT UPON HIM. I HAD OFTEN THOUGHT ABOUT THAT MARK. I REALIZE NOW THAT IN SOME WAY IT WAS A SIGN THAT WOULD PLACE FEAR IN " ANY " MAN, ANIMAL, OR BEAST! WHAT COULD IT HAVE BEEN? WHAT EVER IT WAS I THINK CLEARLY SAID " PROPERTY OF THE LORD ". MAYBE IT WAS THIS " FEAR OF THE LORD " THAT SEPERATED " THE SONS OF GOD " FROM THE OTHER TYPE(S). DON'T ASK ME, I DON'T KNOW. THERE COULD BE THREE TYPES AS FAR AS I KNOW. THE CLUES SAY THAT THERE ARE DEFINITALLY TWO TYPES. TYPE ONE ARE THOSE WHO FEAR GOD. THAT IS SAID AT **www.acts17-11.com/fear.html**: >

THE FEAR OF GOD

Jer 5:22 (NIV) "Should you not fear me?" declares the Lord. "Should you not tremble in my presence?"

See also < clues:FMCJR >

- Serpent (Bible) - Serpent symbolism - Caduceus < clue: FMCJR > - Idolatry - Ophites - Naassenes - Rod of Asclepius - Uraeus - Staff of Moses < clue: FMCJR > - Wadjet - Ningishzida - Nāga < clue: FMCJR > - Footnotes:

< I was trying to figure out how I was going to edit this document. When I came to this point looking at the subheadings below, I realized that I was going to leave many parts of some of the searches in the document. Due to the way that the computer works, I may have to remove several images. When I do that, I will try to leave a note. >

Deities in the Hebrew Bible - Dragons - Hebrew Bible objects - Legendary serpents - Midian - Moses - Supernatural healing - Mythical animals - Book of Exodus < I need to insert something found on the Wayne Blank at keyway.ca site: What Did The Bronze Serpent Mean by Wayne Blank. The web article starts with: " The bronze serpent (RSV), also known as the bronze snake (NIV) and the serpent of brass (KJV) was made by Moses, at God's command, during the Wilderness Journey. The Israelites had been speaking bitterly against God, to which The Lord responded by sending poisonous snakes among the rebels. The bronze serpent was provided as a visible means for repentant believers to be saved from their sin, and was, as Christ Himself plainly stated (see "Fact Finder" below), symbolic of Someone far greater to come. " To read further see the internet article.

The Bronze Serpent

The bronze serpent was made according to God's instructions < deleted image >:

"From Mount Hor they set out by the way to the Red Sea, to go around the Land of Edom; and the people became impatient on the way. And the people spoke against God and against Moses, "Why have you brought us up out of Egypt to die in the wilderness? For there is no food and no water, and we loathe this worthless food."

"Then The Lord [see Rock Of Ages] sent fiery serpents among the people, and they bit the people, so that many people of Israel died. And the people came to Moses, and said, "We have sinned, for we have spoken against The Lord and against you; pray to The Lord, that he take away the serpents from us." So Moses prayed for the people."

"And The Lord said to Moses, "Make a fiery serpent, and set it on a pole; and everyone who is bitten, when he sees it, shall live." So Moses made a bronze serpent, and set it on a pole; and if a serpent bit any man, he would look at the bronze serpent and live." (Numbers 21:4-9 RSV)

" What Happened To The Bronze Serpent " by Wayne Blank

" Centuries later, the bronze serpent was destroyed because the Israelites had turned it into an idol, in violation of The Second Commandment: ' in the third year of Hoshea son of Elah, king of Israel, Hezekiah the son of Ahaz, king of Judah [see Kings of Israel and Judah], began to reign. He was twenty-five years old when he began to reign, and he reigned twenty-nine years in Jerusalem. His mother's name was Abi the daughter of Zechariah." "And he did what was right in the eyes of The Lord, according to all that David [see King David] his father had done. He removed the high places, and broke the pillars, and cut down the Asherah. And he broke in pieces the bronze serpent that Moses had made, for until those days the people of Israel had burned incense to it; it was called Nehushtan." "He trusted in The Lord the God of Israel; so that there was none like him among all the kings of Judah after him, nor among those who were before him. For he held fast to The Lord; he did not depart from following Him, but kept the Commandments [see The Ten Commandments and The Ten Commandments Now?] which The Lord commanded Moses." (2 Kings 18:1-6 RSV). This was included with the subject about Jesus under " **Fact Finder** ": What did Jesus Christ have to say about the symbolism of that bronze serpent? How was the bronze serpent referred-to in regard to one of the most famous verses of the Bible, "For God so loved the world that He gave His only Son, that whoever believes in Him should not perish but have eternal life"?
John 3:14-16

FRANK M. CONAWAY, JR.

YEAR 1857 RAPS

The above ideas come from a sermon (No. 153) < spurgeon.org/index/c03.htm > delivered on Sabbath morning, September 27, 1857, by the Rev. C. H. Spurgen at the Music Hall, Royal Surrey.

JOHN 3:14

"And as Moses lifted up the serpent in the wilderness, even so must the Son of man be lifted up: That whosoever believeth in him should not perish, but have eternal life."—John 3:14. Etc.

PLAY WITH IT

I think that I may be painting the picture that I saw once I had read The Bible for Myself < yes capital M for me , myself, and I >. I have given you what I had read about " wisdom " above. I didn't know that because of the " sins " of the/my forefathers I could be held accountable. I didn't know that I could pass on negative things.

WHAT IS THIS ALL ABOUT I WONDERED

I would like to say that like this:

DAIN'T NOS BODY DONE SAID NATHING

That's right, I haven't **heard** nobody, maybe one, maybe, just fess straight up to it. I can do it. I can do it plain, or I can add some butter. Butter Please. Yelp, as it is written, I came here a sinner. That's what the bible says, so for me that's what it is, period. I repent because, ahh, because I repent that's why! THE END! WOOOSH < 3 points >

SINS OF THE FATHERS:WHEW

Search " the sins of the fathers " on biblestudy tools.com. Searching on the engine comes from " popular resources: Bible Versions, Interlinear Bible, Parallel Bible, Commentaries, Concordances, Dictionaries, Encyclopedias, Lexicons, History, Linking to BST, Bible Verse of the Day, Bible Verses by Topic, Old Testament, New Testament, Sermon Illustrations, Sermon Helps, Bible Reading Plan, Audio Bible ". < THE SALEM WEB NETWORK sites include: **Jesus.org, GodTube.com, LightSource, OnePlace, Crosscards.com, Crosswalk.com,** and **Christianity** >

KUNDALINI DANGER

I think that it is very dangerous to present this type of information without its proper warnings. Sure fire can cook your food, at the same time it can hurt or kill you. You must respect it for what it is! Electric can give many pleasures by powering objects. Sure electric can make life easier, but at the same time it can hurt or even kill you! The same should be said about kundalini. The knowledge of Kundalini can greatly enhance that which is called life. Kundalini is said to be able to open a new meaning to that which is called life, but at the same time the Kundalini is said to greatly destroy that which is not true to the " cause ". Notice that I didn't state what the " cause " is!

DANGER KUNDALINI LEADS TO KRISHNA

The second part of this document is what is so dangerous. At this point I have a few problems with Dr. Bynum's book " DARK LIGHT CONSCIOUSNESS – MELANIN, SERPENT POWER, AND THE LUMINOUS MATRIX OF REALITY " ISBN # 978-159477472-0. On page 224 a comment is given about the " caduceus " symbol. I think that this concept is wrong, although I have seen what should be the correct answer at another place in the book. The book seems like a very advanced cut and paste piece of artwork. This document is so dangerous because it is placed upon a sturdy foundation. Going back to comments by Gopi Krishna on pages 224 - 225, he describes his kundalini opening as " a subtle, organic, nerve like substance in his experience that he perceived as a subtle light coming from the inner lining of his organs – including his stomach, intestines, spleen, kidneys, liver, and lungs, towards his sexual organs – merging there with his

cerebrospinal fluid and then moving in a white – silvery, serpentine motion upward toward his brain, where it eventually emptied, completely submerging and intuition he had of his former self in a radiant, intelligent, astonishingly blissful light. " I find this whole comment not only somewhat strange, but just plain old strange. There use to be a show on television called Soul Train. They had a disco scramble board where contestants would spell names from letters on the board. When the contestants started, the letters were all scrambled up. I fell that each letter is like a particular concept of the kundalini sequence. All the letters have to be used. The question is the sequence correct? First, I say that the sequence is incorrect. Second, I say that how some of the terms, while related to kundalini, were used in the wrong manor. As I understand it, Kundalini Yoga is the highest form of the yoga sciences. There is a reason that there is a spiritual part of the training. The warnings given by the yoga masters are not to be taken lightly!

LIGHT BODY MASS

Third, I think that the final critique of the whole kundalini event is wrong, even to concluding with his " inner light " concept! Even Einstein could conclude that the or a human body has a certain amount of light in it. Does a human body from the time of birth have mass? Look up pound on Wikipedia and you will find < MIND LOOP FROM ABOVE COMENTS >

ADD THE POEM PAGE 285

WIKIPEDIA OF GOPI (KRISHNA)

FRANK M. CONAWAY, JR.

Gopi Krishna (30 May 1903 – 1984) of India as a yogi, mystic, teacher, social reformer, and writer. His autobiography is known under the title Kundalini: The Evolutionary Energy in Man.

Early life

Gopi Krishna was born in 1903, near the city of Srinagar, in the Jammu and Kashmir State in northern India. He spent his earlier years there and later, in Lahore, in the Punjab of British India. At the age of twenty, he returned to Kashmir. During the succeeding years he secured a post in the state government, married and raised a family. Early in his career he became the leader of a social organization that was devoted to helping the disadvantaged in his community, especially with regard to issues concerning the well-being and rights of women.

In 1967 he published his first major book in India, Kundalini—The Evolutionary Energy in Man (currently available under the title Living with Kundalini). Shortly thereafter it was published in Great Britain and the United States and has since appeared in eleven major languages. The book presented his own autobiographical account of the phenomenon of the forceful awakening of Kundalini.

At the age of thirty-four, while meditating one morning, he reported to have experienced the sudden and forceful awakening of Kundalini. In Kundalini: The Evolutionary Energy in Man, he describes what happened: "The illumination grew brighter and brighter, the roaring louder, I experienced a rocking sensation and then felt myself slipping out of my body, entirely enveloped in a halo of light...I felt the point of consciousness that was myself growing wider, surrounded by waves of light...I was now all consciousness, without any outline, without any idea of a corporeal appendage, without any feeling or sensation coming from the senses, immersed in a sea of light simultaneously conscious and aware of every point, spread out, as it were, in all directions without any barrier or material obstruction...bathed in light and in a state of exaltation and happiness impossible to describe."

Gopi Krishna's experience radically altered the path of his life. He came to believe that the human brain was evolving and that an individual's profound mystical experience was a foretaste of what would eventually become an all-pervasive transformation in human consciousness. By his own account, Gopi Krishna's initial experience triggered a transformative process that lasted for twelve years. During this time, the sensations of light, splendor and joy alternated with – and were often completely overshadowed by – sensations of fire, unbearable heat and bleak depression.

FRANK M. CONAWAY, JR.

Before his death in 1984 at the age of eighty-one, Gopi Krishna would write seventeen books on Higher Consciousness – three of them entirely in verse. He credited this output not to his own efforts but to inspiration from a higher source.

One of the little-known facts about Gopi Krishna's life is that he was a crusader for women's rights. Putting this in historical and cultural context shows how very extraordinary his dedication to this cause was. In 1930 it had been less than ten years since women had won the vote and the vast majority of the women in the world were still considered chattel. In India conditions for women were even worse and a man campaigning publicly for women's rights would have been unheard of.

Gopi Krishna was reported to be a supporter for the equality of men and women. He acted, and at one point ended up imprisoned for his actions. One of his most far-reaching contributions involved bettering conditions for widows. At that time in India, the plight of a woman whose husband died was often horrific, especially if she had no grown children to help or protect her. The custom of suttee (throwing oneself on the husband's funeral **pyre**) though outlawed was still practiced, particularly in remote areas.

Along with his humanitarian efforts, Gopi Krishna produced poetry and books in prose and verse form. But his main thrust over the years was to write about mystical experience and the evolution of consciousness from a scientific point of view – that there is supposed to be a biological mechanism in the human body, known from ancient times in India as Kundalini, which is responsible for creativity, genius, psychic ability, religious and mystical experience, as well as some types of aberrant mental illness.

Additional Information

Born in a small village outside Srinagar, Kashmir, Gopi Krishna was one of the first people to popularize the concept of Kundalini among Western readers. His autobiography is entitled Kundalini: The Evolutionary Energy in Man later renamed to Living with Kundalini.[1] According to June McDaniel, his writings have influenced Western interest in kundalini yoga.[2]

He chose the path of yoga due to his circumstances. His father renounced the world to lead a religious life leaving his twenty-eight-year-old mother with the responsibility of raising him and his two sisters. His mother now pinned all her hopes for success on her only son.[3] Pandit Gopi Krishna was also a good freestyle wrestler and it is well known that he beat many a good wrestler. People who knew him well mention that he had the capability to be a world class wrestler, however, he spent most of his energy on intellectual pursuits.

But he failed to pass the examination to enter college, and he now took a lowly job and established his family. He also started on a discipline of meditation to discover who he was.

FRANK M. CONAWAY, JR.

GOPI KRISHNA'S KUNDALINI EXPERIENCE

After having been engaged in this for many years, he had his first Kundalini experience at the age of 34, which he describes thus in his autobiography:[4][5]

> **Suddenly, with a roar like that of a waterfall, I felt a stream of liquid light entering my brain through the spinal cord.**

> **Entirely unprepared for such a development, I was completely taken by surprise; but regaining my self-control, keeping my mind on the point of concentration. The illumination grew brighter and brighter, the roaring louder, I experienced a rocking sensation and then felt myself slipping out of my body, entirely enveloped in a halo of light. It is impossible to describe the experience accurately. I felt the point of consciousness that was myself growing wider surrounded by waves of light. It grew wider and wider, spreading outward while the body, normally the immediate object of its perception, appeared to have receded into the distance until I became entirely unconscious of it. I was now all consciousness without any outline, without any idea of corporeal appendage, without any feeling or sensation coming from the senses, immersed in a sea of light simultaneously conscious and aware at every point, spread out, as it were, in all directions without any barrier or material obstruction. I was no longer myself, or to be more accurate, no longer as I knew myself to be, a small point of awareness confined to a body, but instead was a vast circle of consciousness in which the body was but a point, bathed in light and in a state of exultation and happiness impossible to describe.**

According to June McDaniel, his writings have influenced Western interest in kundalini yoga.[6] He wrote many books and traveled all over the world giving lectures. He came to feel the kundalini experience underlies all (or most) religions that started with a personal revelation. He could see kundalini iconography in cultures worldwide, from ancient Egypt to Quetzalcoatl to the caduceus of Mercury, and believed there was a common basis, and that he had been granted entry to this vision. Gopi Krishna theorized that the brain was in a state of organic evolution, and that the rising of Kundalini into the brain would open a normally silent chamber called brahma-randra in the yogic tradition. Krishna worked tirelessly to promote the scientific investigation of kundalini in the human frame, hypothesizing that this energy was leading humankind towards the goal of higher consciousness.[7]

Research of genius and enlightened persons

In the light of Pandit Gopi Krishna's experiences he himself has started to search the life of geniuses and enlightened persons in history for clues of kundalini awakening. He proposed an organization to be erected to conduct scientific research on the matter.

FRANK M. CONAWAY, JR.

The research should, according to him, consist of research on biological processes in the body, psychological and sociological research of living persons. According to Mr. Krishna the lives of historical persons should also be investigated.[8][9]

One organization has picked up the wish of Mr. Krishna to further investigate the lives of saints, geniuses and inspired people, namely the **Institute for Consciousness Research**.

Notes

1. ^ Krishna, Gopi (1971) Kundalini: the evolutionary energy in man. Boulder, Colorado: Shambhala
2. ^ For quotation "Western interest at the popular level in kundalini yoga was probably most influenced by the writings of Gopi Krishna, in which kundalini was redefined as chaotic and spontaneous religious experience." see: McDaniel, p. 280.
3. ^ Krishna, Gopi (1993)Living with Kundalini: (Shambhala, 1993 ISBN 0-87773-947-1) page 81
4. ^ Krishna, Gopi (1993)Living with Kundalini: (Shambhala, 1993 ISBN 0-87773-947-1)
5. ^ Excerpts from Living with Kundalini on Ecomall
6. ^ For quotation "Western interest at the popular level in kundalini yoga was probably most influenced by the writings of Gopi Krishna, in which kundalini was redefined as chaotic and spontaneous religious experience." see: McDaniel, June. Offering Flowers, Feeding Skulls Popular Goddess Worship in West Bengal. (Oxford University Press, 2006, ISBN 0-19-516791-0) p. 280.
7. ^ An interview with Gopi Krishna
8. ^ Krishna, Gopi (1975). The Dawn of a New Science. New Delhi: Kundalini Research and Publication Trust. ISBN 0-917776-14-3.
9. ^ Last interview with Gopi Krishna

See also

- Consciousness, Enlightenment (spiritual), Kundalini: The Evolutionary Energy in Man, Prakasa, Prana, Qi, Shakti

References

- Krishna, Gopi (1975). The Dawn of a New Science. Institute for Consciousness Research. ISBN 0-917776-14-3.
- McDaniel, June (2006). Offering Flowers, Feeding Skulls Popular Goddess Worship in West Bengal. Oxford University Press. ISBN 0-19-516791-0.
- Krishna, Gopi (1993). Living with Kundalini. Shambhala. ISBN 0-87773-947-1.

FRANK M. CONAWAY, JR.

Further reading[edit]

- Gopi Krishna, Kundalini: The Evolutionary Energy in Man, Shambhala Books, 1970. autobiography

- Yoga: A Vision of its Future, New Delhi: KRPT, 1978.
- Secrets of Kundalini in Panchastivai New Delhi: KRPT, 1976
- The Awakening of Kundalini, New York: E P Dutton, 1975.
- The Real Nature of Mystical Experience, New York: New Concepts Publishing, 1978.
- The Shape of Events to Come, New York: KRPT, 1979. A warning of possible impending nuclear holocaust, in essay and verse.
- The Riddle of Consciousness, New York: Kundalini Research Foundation, 1976. ISBN 0-917776-00-3, entirely in verse.
- The Biological Basis of Religion and Genius, New York: Harper and Row, intro. by Carl Friedrich Freiherr von Weizsäcker, which is half the book, 1971, 1972.
- The Secret of Yoga, New York: Harper and Row, 1972.
- Higher Consciousness: The Evolutionary Thrust of Kundalini, New York: Julian Press, 1974.
- William Irwin Thompson, Passages about Earth: An Exploration of the New Planetary Culture, New York: Harper and Row, 1974. one chapter describes his interaction with Gopi Krishna
- Heehs, Peter (2002). Indian Religions: A Historical Reader of Spiritual Expression and Experience. New York: New York University Press. ISBN 0-8147-3650-5.
- Reichenberg-Ullman, Judyth; Robert Ullman (2001). Mystics, Masters, Saints, and Sages: Stories of Enlightenment. Berkeley, Calif: Conari Press. pp. 155–163. ISBN 1-57324-507-0.

External links

A collection of links related to Gopi Krishna

General info on Gopi Krishna en Kundalini
Retrieved from
"http://en.wikipedia.org/w/index.php?title=Gopi_Krishna_(yogi)&oldid=575407914"
Categories: Yogis, Kashmiri people, Indian writers, Hindu mystics, 1903 births, 1984 deaths, Indian autobiographers, People from Srinagar district

Hidden categories: Articles lacking reliable references from July 2007, All articles lacking reliable references

KUNDALINI: THE EVOLUTIONARY ENERGY IN MAN – WIKIPEDIA, THE

Kundalini: The Evolutionary Energy in Man is the autobiography of Pandit Gopi Krishna. It was originally published in 1967. Later it was renamed Living with Kundalini and is one of the many books that Gopi Krishna wrote about his experience with Kundalini and the subsequent effects of and transformation in mind and body.

Contents: 1 Overview, 2 New self, 3 Today, 4 Physio-Kundalini syndrome, 5 Publication data, 6 References

Gopi Krishna begins the book in his living room Christmas time of 1937. As was his habit in the morning, Krishna "sat steadily, unmoving and erect, my thoughts uninterruptedly centered on the shining lotus".[citation needed] Krishna had been an unsupervised practitioner of meditation for many years, however on this day he experienced what is called a Kundalini Rising or Kundalini Awakening. In many Indian and eastern yogic traditions, Kundalini awakening is the process through which enlightenment is attained. Krishna describes the feeling of his awakening as, "a roar like that of a waterfall, I felt a stream of liquid light entering my brain through the spinal cord" (12). Though Krishna originally doubted the validity of his experience, a repeat experience later that day convinced him of the reality of this development. Though Krishna's development is often held with the highest of praise, he instead felt only depression and anxiety. And it was the beginning of a nearly 25 year struggle to regain his mental, physical and psychic facilities.

Before telling of his struggle with the aftermath of his Kundalini awakening, Krishna gives us a description of Prana and the Nadi (yoga) indicating that Kundalini results in an increase of prana, or the Subtle Energy which controls and regulates all bodily functions. The danger of turning up the voltage soon became apparent to Krishna a few days after his awakening. He portrays his sensations with painful images like "a jet of molten copper...dashed against my crown" (50). He was sick and tired and felt awful. About two months after awakening Kundalini, Krishna believed he was about to die. He had been in agonizing pain for hours, and had barely eaten or slept since his first experience. In his last throws of pain he had a thought; perhaps Kundalini had risen up the pingala instead of the central nadi sushumna. Focusing all his attention he forced Kundalini through the sushumna, saving his life. Krishna felt the burning pain cease, and burning flame in his skull was replaced by blissful radiance.

Once Kundalini had been correctly risen in Krishna, he now experienced many "strange sounds and strange lights; but the current was now warm and pleasing instead of hot and burning" (84). Over time, he was able to restore his strength and mental clarity. His journey however was long and strenuous. For years Krishna struggled to find the balance between his now extremely delicate and fragile body and the demands of his life. He had to balance diet, exercise, and his mental strain in order to remain healthy; Often the slightest deviation was reprimanded by extreme discomfort and pain. In the end, Krishna succeeds in finding his balance of body, mind, and spirit. His experience with the "superconscious", which is similar to Carl Jung's collective unconscious began more than a decade after his awakening led Krishna to share his story and his experience with Kundalini to the world. Opening the doors of ancient practices to the minds of present people all over the world.

New self

In all forms of religious and spiritual development and practice, the goal is always the formation of a new self. In the book Krishna describes just that process in detail. He was simply going through his life working in a government building, he was content, but he had decided years ago to adhere to a strict path of sobriety and the practice of meditation. It was this will that led Krishna down the path to awakening Kundalini. After his accidental awakening, and severe physical anguish, Krishna learns that his body is going through major changes in efficiently and connections within the body to other organs and glands. After years of careful eating and resting habits, the changes that he begins to describe are less about physical changes and are now about the changes that he is going through in his mind. After the awakening Krishna lost all desire in the supernatural, he was simply repulsed by meditation. Then, when the time came in his development to reform the mind Krishna had to test and begin to understand how his mental and psychic abilities were being augmented. This too when strained too hard or rubbed incorrectly caused Krishna physical and mental suffering, yet over time he too was able to find a new mental normalcy. **Then came time for the last step, the path up towards enlightenment**.

Twelve years after Krishna's awakening, we begin to hear about the bliss and the wonderful luminosity that he had not felt since the first awakening of Kundalini. But now, Krishna explains the complexity of his sensations and feelings in metaphor. This method of allegory and symbolism appears to be the only way to grasp such states of consciousness.[1] In Krishna's daily life he begins to feel, "like a sentient dewdrop floating intact in an ocean of pure being without mingling with the surrounding water" (199). Shortly after these feelings present themselves, Krishna has the inclination to begin writing poetry. Though he had no experience and his verses were poor he persisted, about a month later he was walking on the street when **suddenly he became lost in his own mind**, completely detached from his physical surrounding. It was then that two perfectly formed lines of poetry came out of the ether in his native tongue Kashmiri. His excitement became more apparent and amazed when over the next few weeks he received poems in English, Persian, Punjabi, German, French, Italian and Arabic. What was so incredible was that he had never heard nor read anything in German, French, or many of the later languages. Where did these poems come from?

Along with the sudden development of receiving messages from the superconscious, Krishna also began to be extremely altruistic. This process is seen very often with those that reach enlightenment. The story of man leaving all behind to climb the symbolic mountain, reaching the mountain and attaining enlightenment is always followed by the enlightened traveling back down the mountain to help those on the ground. Within mysticism altruism is never too far away, especially in the advanced or later stages of the journey. Swami Akhilananda argues that it is the realization that the divine is in all living things, in animals, plants, and man that creates the desire for altruism. The result of this desire for increased well-being of fellow man often compels the enlightened individual to pursue some form of altruistic work.[2] This is the story of Moses, and the symbols are repeated throughout history. And Krishna repeats this story not just by helping those people around him, but by creating these books and writings that have guided many others towards the path of kundalini.

With the help of Krishna and others, the Western World has been introduced to the idea of subtle energy and the effects of meditation on the mind and body.[3] As Krishna wished to show in all of his books, Kundalini awakening and the subsequent changes in the physical and mental bodies is not a psychosomatic or unnatural event. Instead Kundalini awakening is a very scientific and biological event in the body. Today research done in the mind and consciousness seem to be coming closer to this understanding. They can see that there are marked physical differences in those men and women who have consistently practiced meditation.[4] Today there are many classes and groups helping with awakening Kundalini and the traditional methods as well. One of the most famous classes is Hoshin Roshi Ryu previously led by Glenn Morris who created the Improved K.A.P (Kundalini Awakening Process) which has been used by hundreds of individuals without any of the pain and imbalance that Krishna survived.

Physio-Kundalini syndrome

In the 1980s a bioengineer named Itzhak Bentov created a model of a physiological process that could be used to help the medical world understand the physiological effects of kundalini.[5] **Bentov, as well as many other scientists at the time believe that meditation or other more physical experiences such as near death experiences could also force the body into awaken Kundalini. The body, "attempts a last-ditch life-saving effort by empowering and directing the bodies prana to flow directly into the brain; this overwhelming rush of potent energy produces the visions and other phenomenon typical of NDEs.[6]** In fact this knowledge was also known to the ancients of India, one group actually practiced **tongue-swallowing** as a catalyst to forcing Kundalini up into the brain.[7] Research of this type into the biological effects and processes of Kundalini, and in meditation help to blend the Eastern and Western practices of health and wellness together creating a larger and more complete picture.

FRANK M. CONAWAY, JR.

Publication data[edit]

- Krishna, Gopi. Kundalini: The Evolutionary Energy in Man. Boston: Shambhala, 1970. Print.

References[edit]

1. ^ Albanese, Catherine L. "The Subtle Energies of Spirit: Explorations in Metaphysical and New Age Spirituality." Journal of the American Academy of Religion 67.2 (1999): 305–25. Print.
2. ^ Akhilananda, Swami. "Mysticism and Altruism." Journal of Bibal and Religion 16.2 (1948): 89–93. Print.
3. ^ Rosch, Paul J. "Bioelectromagnetic and Subtle Energy Medicine." Annals of the New York Academy of Sciences 1172 (2009): 297–311. Print.
4. ^ Lefevere, Patricia. "Fanning the fire of qi: monk builds bridges between East and West, science and spirituality.(RELIGIOUS LIFE)(Bernard Seif)." National Catholic Reporter 43.17 (2003). Print.
5. ^ Greyson, Bruce. "Near-Death Experiences and the Physio-Kundalini Syndrome." Journal of Religion and Health 32.4 (1993): 277–90. Print.
6. ^ Kieffer, G. "The Near-Death Experience and Kundalini." J. Near-Death Studies. Print.
7. ^ Greyson op. cit.

Retrieved from
"http://en.wikipedia.org/w/index.php?title=Kundalini:_The_Evolutionary_Energy_in_Man&oldid=578329846"
Categories: 1967 books, Religious autobiographies, Vitalism, Yoga texts and documentation

Hidden categories: Articles needing additional references from March 2013, All articles needing additional references, All articles with unsourced statements, Articles with unsourced statements from October 2013, Wikipedia articles that may have off-topic sections < Relates to The Book of The Revelation >

WIKIPEDIA JONAH: JONAH IN CHRISTIANITY

From Wikipedia, the free encyclopedia, I would add a few of its comments.

" **Jonah** or **Jonas** (Hebrew, Modern Yona Tiberian Yona; dove; Arabic: Yunus, Yunis or Yunan ; Greek/Latin: Ionas) is the name given in the Hebrew Bible (Tanakh/Old Testament) to a prophet of the northern kingdom of Israel in about the 8th century BC, the eponymous central character in the Book of Jonah, famous for being swallowed by a fish or a whale, depending on translation. The Biblical story of Jonah is also repeated, with a few notable differences, in the Qur'an. " "

Jonah in sailors' superstition

A long-established expression among sailors uses the term "a Jonah" as meaning a person (either a sailor or a passenger) whose presence on board brings bad luck and endangers the ship.[16] Later on, this meaning was extended to "a Jonah" referring to "a person who carries a jinx, one who will bring bad luck to any enterprise."[17]

The fish < image deleted >
Depiction of Jonah and the "great fish" on the south doorway of the Gothic-era Dom St. Peter in Worms, Germany.

Interpretations of the "fish" fall into these general categories:[18]

1. A big fish or whale (of unspecified species) did indeed swallow Jonah.
2. A special creation (not any fish we know of) of God accomplished the act.
3. There was no fish: the story is an allegory, the fish is a literary device in the story, the story is a vision or a dream etc.

Translation

Though it is often called a whale today, the Hebrew, as throughout scripture, refers to no species in particular, simply sufficing with "great fish" or "big fish" (whales are today classified as mammals and not fish, but no such distinction was made in antiquity). While some Bible scholars suggest the size and habits of the great white shark correspond better to the representations given of Jonah's being swallowed, normally an adult human is too large to be swallowed whole.[19]

In Jonah 2:1 (1:17 in English translation), the original Hebrew text reads dag gadol (גדול דג), which literally means "big fish." The Septuagint translates this phrase into Greek as ketos megas (κητος μεγας). The term ketos alone means "huge fish," and in Greek mythology the term was closely associated with sea monsters, including sea serpents.[20] Jerome later translated this phrase as piscis granda in his Latin Vulgate. He translated ketos, however, as cetus in Matthew 12:40.

At some point cetus became synonymous with "whale" (the study of whales is now called cetology). In his 1534 translation, William Tyndale translated the phrase in Jonah 2:1 as "greate fyshe" and he translated the word ketos (Greek) or cetus (Latin) in Matthew 12:40 as "whale". Which states "For as Jonas was three days and three nights in the whale's belly; so shall the Son of man be three days and three nights in the heart of the earth."[21] Tyndale's translation was later incorporated into the Authorized Version of 1611. Since then, the "great fish" in Jonah 2 has been most often interpreted as a whale.

In Turkish, "Jonah fish" (in Turkish yunus baligi) is the word used for dolphin, often shortened to just yunus.

Suggested literal interpretations

Some believers claim that God, being omnipotent, simply altered things as needed and sustained Jonah - the same as in other miraculous accounts in the Hebrew scriptures. Some believers claim that Jonah did die in the belly of the great fish, and was then resurrected by God since Jesus himself associated this event in Jonah's life with his own death and resurrection. See Matthew 12:40. Others have attempted more elaborate explanations.

As for a fish or whale that could repeat the feat of swallowing a human being whole, several candidates have been suggested. The largest whales - baleen whales, a group which includes the blue whale - eat plankton and "it is commonly said that this species would be choked if it attempted to swallow a herring."[22] As for the whale shark, Dr. E. W. Gudger, an Honorary Associate in Ichthyology at the American Museum of Natural History, noted that "while the mouth is cavernous, the throat itself is only four inches wide and has a sharp elbow or bend behind the opening. This gullet would not permit the passage of a man's arm"[citation needed]. In another publication he also noted that "the whale shark is not the fish that swallowed Jonah."[23][24]

Connections to other legends

Joseph Campbell suggested a parallel between the story of Jonah and the epic of Gilgamesh, in which Gilgamesh obtains a plant from the bottom of the sea.[26] In the Book of Jonah a worm (in Hebrew tola'ath, "maggot") bites the shade-giving plant's root causing it to wither, while in the epic of Gilgamesh, Gilgamesh plucks his plant from the floor of the sea which he reached by tying stones to his feet. Once he makes it back to the shore, the rejuvenating plant is eaten by a serpent.

Campbell also noted several similarities between the story of Jonah and that of Jason in Greek mythology. The Greek rendering of the name Jonah was Jonas, which differs from Jason only in the order of sounds—both os are omegas suggesting that Jason was confused with Jonah. Gildas Hamel, drawing on the Book of Jonah and Greco-Roman sources — including Greek vases and the accounts of Apollonius of Rhodes, Gaius Valerius Flaccus and Orphic Argonautica—[27] identifies a number of shared motifs, including the names of the heroes, the presence of a dove, the idea of "fleeing" like the wind and causing a storm, the attitude of the sailors, the presence of a sea-monster or dragon threatening the hero or swallowing him, and the form and the word used for the "gourd" (kikayon). Hamel takes the view that it was the Hebrew author who was reacting to and adapting this mythological material to communicate his own, quite different message. The Greek sources are however several centuries later than the Book of Jonah and the form Jonas which is similar to Jason is from the Septuagint translation of the book.

Biblical scholars have speculated that Jonah may have been in part the inspiration behind the figure of Oannes in late Babylonian mythology.[28] The deity name "Oannes" first occurs in texts from the Library of Ashurbanipal (more than a century after the time of Jonah) as Uanna or Uan but is assimilated to Adapa, a deity first mentioned on fragments of tablets from the 15th or 14th century B.C. found in Amarna in Egypt.[29][30] Oannes is described as dwelling in the Persian Gulf, and rising out of the waters in the daytime and furnishing mankind instruction in writing, the arts and the various sciences. Berossus describes Oannes as having the body of a fish but underneath the figure of a man—a detail that, some Biblical scholars[who?] suggest, is not derived from Adapa but is perhaps based on a misinterpretation of images of Jonah emerging from the fish. Scholars of Mesopotamian mythology, however, suggest that Adapa was likely associated with fishing and depicted in half-fish form many centuries before the story of Jonah appeared.[29] Nineteenth-century Irish amateur scholar William Betham speculated that worship of Oannes is the origin of the cult of the Roman god Janus.[31]

Jonah is mentioned twice in Chapter 14 of the apocryphal Book of Tobit, the conclusion of which finds Tobit's son, Tobias, at the extreme age of one hundred and twenty seven years, rejoicing at the news of Nineveh's destruction by Nebuchadnezzar and Ahasuerus in apparent fulfillment of Jonah's prophecy against the Assyrian capital.

MORE JONAH
External links: Wikimedia Commons has media related to Jonah. The Book of Jonah (Hebrew and English), The Book of Jonah (NIV), Jewish Encyclopedia: Jonah, Catholic Encyclopedia: Jonah, Prophet Jonah Orthodox icon and synaxarion, Animated Retelling of the Jonah Story.

Retrieved from "http://en.wikipedia.org/w/index.php?title=Jonah&oldid=582712389" Categories: Prophets of the Hebrew Bible, Christian saints from the Old Testament, People celebrated in the Lutheran liturgical calendar, Fertile Crescent, Jonah, Muslim views of biblical figures, Prophets of Islam, Abrahamic mythology, Interactions between humans and fish.

FRANK M. CONAWAY, JR.

SIGN OF JONAS = JONAH

TYPOLOGY (THEOLOGY) – WIKIPEDIA: GO TO EXAMPLE OF JONAH

From Wikipedia, the free encyclopedia. < image deleted: The Ascension from a Speculum Humanae Salvationis ca. 1430, see below. >

Typology in Christian theology and Biblical exegesis is a doctrine or theory concerning the predictive relationship of the Old Testament to the New Testament. Events, persons or statements in the Old Testament are seen as **types** pre-figuring or superseded by **antitypes**, events or aspects of Christ or his revelation described in the New Testament. For example Jonah may be seen as the **type** of Christ in that he appeared to have emerged from the whale's belly and from death. In the fullest version of the theory of typology, the whole purpose of the Old Testament is viewed as merely the provision of types for Christ, the antitype, or fulfillment. The theory began in the Early Church, was at its most influential in the High Middle Ages, and continued to be popular, especially in Calvinism, after the Protestant Reformation, but in subsequent periods has been given less emphasis.[1] The most notable exception to this is in the Eastern Orthodox Church, where typology is still a common and frequent exegetical tool, mainly due to that church's great emphasis on continuity in doctrinal presentation through all historical periods. Typology was frequently used in early Christian art, where type and antitype would be depicted in contrasting positions. The usage of the terminology has expanded into the secular sphere, as in for example "Geoffrey de Montbray (d.1093), Bishop of Coutances, a right-hand man of William the Conqueror, was a type of the great feudal prelate, warrior and administrator". [2]

Contents: 1 Etymology, 2 Origin of the theory, 3 Development of typology, 3.1 Example of Jonah, 4 Other Old Testament examples, 4.1 Sacrifice of Isaac, 4.2 Joseph, 4.3 Moses, 4.4 Inanimate types, 5 Post-biblical usage, 6 See also, 7 Bibliography, 8 References, and 9 External links

Etymology

The term derives from the Greek noun τύπος (typos, pron. "teepos"), "a blow, hitting, stamp", and thus the figure or impression made on a coin etc. by such action, that is an image, figure or statue of a man; also an original pattern, model or mould < I LEFT THIS IN FOR A REASON THAT MAKES SENSE OF A THEORY ABOUT CREATION AND THE LIGHT TO ME >. To this is prefixed the Greek preposition anti meaning opposite, corresponding.[3][4]

Origin of the theory

The Early Christians, in considering the Old Testament, needed to decide what its role and purpose was for them, given that Christian revelation and the New Covenant might be considered to have superseded it, and many specific Old Testament rules and requirements in books such as Leviticus dealing with Expounding of the Law were no longer being followed. [5] One purpose of the Old Testament for Christians was to demonstrate that the Ministry of Jesus and Christ's first coming had been prophesied and foreseen, and the Gospels indeed were seen to contain many quotations from the Old Testament which explicitly and implicitly link Jesus to Old Testament prophecies. Typology greatly extended the number of these links by adding to Old Testament prophecies fulfilled by Christ others based on the mere similarity of Old Testament actions or situations to an aspect of Christ.

Typology is also a theory of history, seeing the whole story of the Jewish and Christian peoples as shaped by God, with events within the story acting as symbols for later events - in this role God is often compared to a writer, using actual events instead of fiction to shape his narrative.[6]

Development of typology

The system of Medieval allegory began in the Early Church as a method for synthesizing these seeming discontinuities between the Hebrew Bible (Old Testament) and the New Testament. While the Church studied both testaments and saw each as equally inspired by God, the Old Testament contained discontinuities for Christians, for example, the Jewish kosher laws and the requirement for male circumcision. The Old Testament could therefore be seen in places not as a literal account, but as an allegory, or foreshadowing, of the events of the New Testament, in particular how the events of the Old Testament related to the events of Christ's life. Most theorists believed in the literal truth of the Old Testament accounts, but regarded the events described as shaped by God to provide types foreshadowing Christ. Others regarded some parts of the Bible as essentially allegorical; however the typological relationships remain the same whichever view is taken. The doctrine is stated by Paul in Colossians 2:16-17 - "Therefore do not let anyone judge you by what you eat or drink, or with regard to a religious festival, a New Moon celebration or a sabbath day. These are a shadow of the things that were to come; the reality, however, is found in Christ." It also finds expression in the Letter to the Hebrews.

The development of this as a systematic view of the Hebrew Bible was influenced by the thought of the Hellenistic Jewish world centered in Alexandria, where Philo and others viewed the Bible in philosophical terms (contemporary Greek literary theory highlighted foreshadowing as a literary device), as essentially an allegory - borrowing some Platonic concepts from their Pagan neighbors. Origen Christianized the system , and figures including Hilary of Poitiers and Ambrose spread it. Saint Augustine (345-530) recalled often hearing Ambrose say that "the letter kills but the spirit gives life" and he in turn became a hugely influential proponent of the system, though also insisting on the literal historical truth of the Bible. Isidore of Seville (ca. 560-636) and Rabanus Maurus (ca. 780-856) became influential as summarizers and compilers of works setting out standardized interpretations of correspondences and their meanings.[7] Jewish typological thought has continued to develop in Rabbinic literature, including the Kabbalah, with concepts like the Pardes or four approaches to a Biblical text.

Typology frequently emerged in art; many typological pairings appear in sculpture on cathedrals and churches, and in other media. Popular illustrated works expounding typological couplings were among the commonest books of the late Middle Ages, as illuminated manuscripts, blockbooks, and incunabula (early printed books). The two most successful compilations were the Speculum Humanae Salvationis and the Biblia pauperum'.

Example of Jonah

An example of typology is the story of Jonah and the fish from the Old Testament. In the Old Testament Jonah told the men aboard the ship to sacrifice him by throwing him overboard. Jonah told them that by taking his life, God's wrath would pass and the sea would become calm. Subsequently Jonah then spends three days and three nights in the belly of a great fish before he is spat up onto dry land. Typological interpretation of this story holds that it prefigures Christ's burial, the stomach of the fish being Christ's tomb: as Jonah was freed from the fish after three days and three nights, so did Christ rise from His tomb on the third day. In the New Testament Jesus can be thought to invoke Jonah as a type: "As the crowds increased, Jesus said, "This is a wicked generation. It asks for a miraculous sign, but none will be given it except the sign of Jonah." Luke 11:29–32 (see also Matthew 12:38–42, 16:1–4). Jonah called the belly of the fish "She'ol", the land of the dead (translated "the grave" in the NIV).

Thus, whenever one finds an allusion to Jonah in Medieval art or Medieval literature, it is usually an allegory for the burial and resurrection of Christ. Another common typological allegory entails the four major Old testament prophets Isaiah, Jeremiah, Ezekiel, and Daniel prefiguring the four Evangelists Matthew, Mark, Luke, and John, or the twelve tribes of Israel foreshadowing the twelve apostles. There was no end to the number of analogies that commentators could find between stories of the Old Testament and the New; modern typologists prefer to limit themselves to considering typological relationships that they find sanctioned in the New Testament itself, as in the example of Jonah above.[8]

WHICH BIBLE

1550 Stephanus New Testament (BibleGateway)

1881 Westcott-Hort New Testament (BibleGateway)

1894 Scrivener New Testament (BibleGateway)

1934 Vietnamese Bible (BibleGateway)

21st Century King James Version (BibleGateway)

Albanian Bible (BibleGateway)

American Standard Version (BibleGateway)

Amplified Bible (BibleGateway)

Ang Salita ng Diyos (BibleGateway)

Arabic Life Application Bible (BibleGateway)

BibleBrowser.com

BibleCommenter.com (BibleBrowser)

Biblia Sacra Vulgata (BibleGateway)

Biblia en Lenguaje Sencillo (BibleGateway)

Bulgarian Bible (BibleGateway)

Castillian (BibleGateway)

Chinese Union Version (BibleGateway)

Conferenza Episcopale Italiana (BibleGateway)

Contemporary English Version (BibleGateway)

Croatian Bible (BibleGateway)

Darby Translation (BibleGateway)

Det Norsk Bibelselskap 1930 (BibleGateway)

Dette er Biblen (BibleGateway)

Dios Habla Hoy (BibleGateway)

Douay-Rheims 1899 American Edition (BibleGateway)

English Standard Version (BibleGateway)

Greek audio of New Testament (greeklatinaudio.com)

Haitian Creole Version (BibleGateway)

Het Boek (BibleGateway)

Hiligaynon Bible (BibleGateway)

Holman Christian Standard Bible (BibleGateway)

Hungarian KAiroli (BibleGateway)

Icelandic Bible (BibleGateway)

Il Nuovo Testamento in Lingua Moderna (BibleGateway)

João Ferreira de Almeida Atualizada (BibleGateway)

King James Version (BibleGateway)

Korean Bible (BibleGateway)

La Bible du Semeur (BibleGateway)

La Biblia de las Américas (BibleGateway)

La Nuaova Diodati (BibleGateway)

Latin audio of New Testament (greeklatinaudio.com)

Levande Bibeln (BibleGateway)

Louis Segond (BibleGateway)

Luther Bibel 1545 (BibleGateway)

Maori Bible (BibleGateway)

New American Bible (USCCB)

New American Standard Bible (BibleGateway)

New International Reader's Version (BibleGateway)

New International Version (BibleGateway)

New International Version - UK (BibleGateway)

New King James Version (BibleGateway)

New Life Version (BibleGateway)

New Living Translation (BibleGateway)

New Revised Standard Version (Oremus)

Nova Versão Internacional (BibleGateway)

Nueva Versión Internacional (BibleGateway)

Nádej pre kazdého (BibleGateway)

O Livro (BibleGateway)

Online Parallel Bible (bible.cc)

Reimer 2001 (BibleGateway)

Reina-Valera 1960 (BibleGateway)

Reina-Valera 1995 (BibleGateway)

Reina-Valera Antigua (BibleGateway)

Romanian (BibleGateway)

Romanian Cornilescu Version (BibleGateway)

Russian Synodal Version (BibleGateway)

ScriptureText.com multilingual (BibleBrowser)

Slovo Zhizny (BibleGateway)

Slovo na cestu (BibleGateway)

Svenska 1917 (BibleGateway)

Swahili New Testament (BibleGateway)

The Message (BibleGateway)

Worldwide English (New Testament) (BibleGateway)

Wycliffe New Testament (BibleGateway)

Young's Literal Translation (BibleGateway)

LET'S LOOK CLOSE

I want to give you a few scriptures to look up on " biblehub.com "or " biblestudytools.com ". I might as well get right to the point. Look up Luke 11:21on biblehub.com. Now look at the New Living Translation. The verse says like who? Now compare it to the rest of the bibles. See what I mean? You might want to check Luke 11:20 – 32, Matthew 12:38-42, Deuteronomy 3:11, and Revelation 13:18. Sometimes you have to look close. You might even find something funny.

WOMAN WHAT

I thought that this was kind of funny. Just imagine that you hear a woman yell out what is said at Luke 11:27. Look at these three versions: the New Living Translation, the GOD'S WORD Translation, and the Weymouth New Testament. Let's use the Weymouth New Testament. The Weymouth New Testament : As He thus spoke a woman in the crowd called out in a loud voice, "Blessed is the mother who carried you, and the breasts that you have sucked." Nah, let's use the New Living Translation. The New Living Translation says: As he was speaking, a woman in the crowd called out, "God bless your mother--the womb from which you came, and the breasts that nursed you!" Here is the funny part. The New Living Translation says "Jesus replied, 'But even more blessed are all who hear the word of God and put it into practice.'" Do you think that is funny or what?

JOHN 21:15 < COMPARE TRANSLATIONS FOR JOHN 21:15 >

John 21:15 ASV

American Standard Version

So when they had broken their fast, Jesus saith to Simon Peter, Simon, [son] of John, lovest thou me more than these? He saith unto him, Yea, Lord; thou knowest that I love thee. He saith unto him, Feed my lambs.

John 21:15 BBE

Bible in Basic English

Then when they had taken food, Jesus said to Simon Peter, Simon, son of John, is your love for me greater than the love of these others? He said to him, Yes, Lord; you are certain of my love for you. He said to him, Then give my lambs food.

John 21:15 CEB

Common English Bible

When they finished eating, Jesus asked Simon Peter, "Simon son of John, do you love me more than these?" Simon replied, "Yes, Lord, you know I love you." Jesus said to him, "Feed my lambs."

John 21:15 CJB

Complete Jewish Bible

After breakfast, Yeshua said to Shim`on Kefa, "Shim`on Bar-Yochanan, do you love me more than these?" He replied, "Yes, Lord, you know I'm your friend." He said to him, "Feed my lambs."

John 21:15 RHE

Douay-Rheims

When therefore they had dined, Jesus saith to Simon Peter: Simon, son of John, lovest thou me more than these? He saith to him: Yea, Lord, thou knowest that I love thee. He saith to him: Feed my lambs.

John 21:15 ESV

English Standard Version

When they had finished breakfast, Jesus said to Simon Peter, "Simon, son of John, do you love me more than these?" He said to him, "Yes, Lord; you know that I love you." He said to him, "Feed my lambs."

John 21:15 GW

GOD'S WORD Translation

FRANK M. CONAWAY, JR.

After they had eaten breakfast, Jesus asked Simon Peter, "Simon, son of John, do you love me more than the other disciples do?" Peter answered him, "Yes, Lord, you know that I love you." Jesus told him, "Feed my lambs."

John 21:15 GNT

Good News Translation

After they had eaten, Jesus said to Simon Peter, "Simon son of John, do you love me more than these others do?" "Yes, Lord," he answered, "you know that I love you." Jesus said to him, "Take care of my lambs."

John 21:15 HNV

Hebrew Names Version

So when they had eaten their breakfast, Yeshua said to Shim`on Kefa, "Shim`on, son of Yonah, do you love me more than these?" He said to him, "Yes, Lord; you know that I have affection for you." He said to him, "Feed my lambs."

John 21:15 CSB

Holman Christian Standard

When they had eaten breakfast, Jesus asked Simon Peter, "Simon, son of John, do you love , the first 2 times by Jesus (vv. 15-16); and phileo , the last time by Jesus (v. 17) and all 3 times by Peter (vv. 15-17). Peter's threefold confession of love for Jesus corresponds to his earlier threefold denial of Jesus; Jn 18:15-18 , 25-27 . Me more than these?" "Yes, Lord," he said to Him, "You know that I love You." "Feed My lambs," He told him.

John 21:15 KJV

King James Version

So when they had dined , Jesus saith to Simon Peter, Simon, son of Jonas, lovest thou me more than these? He saith unto him, Yea, Lord; thou knowest that I love thee. He saith unto him, Feed my lambs.

John 21:15 LEB

Lexham English Bible

Now when they had eaten breakfast, Jesus said to Simon Peter, "Simon [son] of John, do you love me more than these?" He said to him, "Yes, Lord, you know that I love you." He said to him, "Feed my lambs!"

John 21:15 NAS

New American Standard

So when they had finished breakfast, Jesus said to Simon Peter, "Simon, son of John, do you love Me more than these ?" He said to Him, "Yes, Lord ; You know that I love You." He said to him, "Tend My lambs."

Read John 21 NAS | Read John 21:15 NAS in parallel | Interlinear view

John 21:15 NCV

New Century Version

When they finished eating, Jesus said to Simon Peter, "Simon son of John do you love me more than these?" He answered, "Yes, Lord, you know that I love you." Jesus said, "Feed my lambs."

John 21:15 NIRV

New International Reader's Version

When Jesus and the disciples had finished eating, Jesus spoke to Simon Peter. He asked, "Simon, son of John, do you really love me more than these others do?" "Yes, Lord," he answered. "You know that I love you." Jesus said, "Feed my lambs."

John 21:15 NIV

New International Version

When they had finished eating, Jesus said to Simon Peter, "Simon son of John, do you truly love me more than these?" "Yes, Lord," he said, "you know that I love you." Jesus said, "Feed my lambs."

John 21:15 NKJV

New King James Version

So when they had eaten breakfast, Jesus said to Simon Peter, "Simon, son of Jonah, do you love Me more than these?" He said to Him, "Yes, Lord; You know that I love You." He said to him, "Feed My lambs."

John 21:15 NLT

New Living Translation

After breakfast Jesus said to Simon Peter, "Simon son of John, do you love me more than these?" "Yes, Lord," Peter replied, "you know I love you." "Then feed my lambs," Jesus told him.

John 21:15 NRS

New Revised Standard

When they had finished breakfast, Jesus said to Simon Peter, "Simon son of John, do you love me more than these?" He said to him, "Yes, Lord; you know that I love you." Jesus said to him, "Feed my lambs."

John 21:15 RSV

Revised Standard Version

When they had finished breakfast, Jesus said to Simon Peter, "Simon, son of John, do you love me more than these?" He said to him, "Yes, Lord; you know that I love you." He said to him, "Feed my lambs."

John 21:15 DBY

The Darby Translation

When therefore they had dined, Jesus says to Simon Peter, Simon, [son] of Jonas, lovest thou me more than these? He says to him, Yea, Lord; thou knowest that I am attached to thee. He says to him, Feed my lambs.

John 21:15 MSG

The Message

After breakfast, Jesus said to Simon Peter, "Simon, son of John, do you love me more than these?" "Yes, Master, you know I love you." Jesus said, "Feed my lambs."

John 21:15 WBT

The Webster Bible

So when they had dined, Jesus saith to Simon Peter, Simon [son] of Jonas, lovest thou me more than these? He saith to him, Yes, Lord: thou knowest that I love thee. He saith to him, Feed my lambs.

John 21:15 TMB

Third Millennium Bible

So when they had dined, Jesus said to Simon Peter, "Simon, son of Jonah, lovest thou Me more than these?" He said unto Him, "Yea, Lord; Thou knowest that I love Thee." He said unto him, "Feed My lambs."

John 21:15 TNIV

Today's New International Version

When they had finished eating, Jesus said to Simon Peter, "Simon son of John, do you love me more than these?" "Yes, Lord," he said, "you know that I love you." Jesus said, "Feed my lambs."

John 21:15 TYN

Tyndale

When they had dyned Iesus sayde to Simon Peter: Simon Ioana lovest thou me more than these? He sayde vnto him: ye Lorde thou knowest that I love thee. He sayde vnto him: feed my lambs.

John 21:15 WNT

Weymouth New Testament

When they had finished breakfast, Jesus asked Simon Peter, "Simon, son of John, do you love me more than these others do?" "Yes, Master," was his answer; "you know that you are dear to me." "Then feed my lambs," replied Jesus.

John 21:15 WEB

World English Bible

So when they had eaten their breakfast, Jesus said to Simon Peter, "Simon, son of Jonah, do you love me more than these?" He said to him, "Yes, Lord; you know that I have affection for you." He said to him, "Feed my lambs."

John 21:15 WYC

Wycliffe

And when they had eaten, Jesus saith to Simon Peter, Simon of Jonas, lovest thou me more than these? He saith to him, Yea, Lord, thou knowest that I love thee. Jesus saith to him, Feed thou my lambs [Feed my lambs].

John 21:15 YLT

Young's Literal Translation

When, therefore, they dined, Jesus saith to Simon Peter, `Simon, [son] of Jonas, dost thou love me more than these?' he saith to him, `Yes, Lord; thou hast known that I dearly love thee;' he saith to him, `Feed my lambs.'

FRANK M. CONAWAY, JR.

John 21 Commentary - Matthew Henry Commentary on the Whole Bible (Concise)

Chapter 21

Christ appears to his disciples. (1-14) His discourse with Peter. (15-19) Christ's declaration concerning John. (20-24) The conclusion. (25)

Verses 1-14 Christ makes himself known to his people, usually in his ordinances; but sometimes by his Spirit he visits them when employed in their business. It is good for the disciples of Christ to be together in common conversation, and common business. The hour for their entering upon action was not come. They would help to maintain themselves, and not be burdensome to any. Christ's time of making himself known to his people, is when they are most at a loss. He knows the temporal wants of his people, and has promised them not only grace sufficient, but food convenient. Divine Providence extends itself to things most minute, and those are happy who acknowledge God in all their ways. Those who are humble, diligent, and patient, though their labors may be crossed, shall be crowned; they sometimes live to see their affairs take a happy turn, after many struggles. And there is nothing lost by observing Christ's orders; it is casting the net on the right side of the ship. Jesus manifests himself to his people by doing that for them which none else can do, and things which they looked not for. He would take care that those who left all for him, should not want any good thing. And latter favours are to bring to mind former favours, that eaten bread may not be forgotten. He whom Jesus loved was the first that said, It is the Lord. John had cleaved most closely to his Master in his sufferings, and knew him soonest. Peter was the most zealous, and reached Christ the first. How variously God dispenses his gifts, and what difference there may be between some believers and others in the way of their honoring Christ, yet they all may be accepted of him! Others continue in the ship, drag the net, and bring the fish to shore, and such persons ought not to be blamed as worldly; for they, in their places, are as truly serving Christ as the others. The Lord Jesus had provision ready for them. We need not be curious in inquiring whence this came; but we may be comforted at Christ's care for his disciples. Although there were so many, and such great fishes, yet they lost none, nor damaged their net. The net of the gospel has enclosed multitudes, yet it is as strong as ever to bring souls to God.

Verses 15-19 Our Lord addressed Peter by his original name, as if he had forfeited that of Peter through his denying him. He now answered, Thou knowest that I love thee; but without professing to love Jesus more than others. We must not be surprised to have our sincerity called into question, when we ourselves have done that which makes it doubtful. Every remembrance of past sins, even pardoned sins, renews the sorrow of a true penitent. Conscious of integrity, Peter solemnly appealed to Christ, as knowing all things, even the secrets of his heart. It is well when our falls and mistakes make us more humble and watchful. The sincerity of our love to God must be brought to the test; and it behooves us to inquire with earnest, preserving prayer to the heart-searching God, to examine and prove us, whether we are able to stand this test. No one can be qualified to feed the sheep and lambs of Christ, who does not love the good Shepherd more than any earthly advantage or object. It is the great concern of every good man, whatever death he dies, to glorify God in it; for what is our chief end but this, to die to the Lord, at the word of the Lord?

WHAT IS THIS TO US

< I HAD TO ADD THIS FOR THE CHRISTIAN MINDSET >?

Verses 20-24 Sufferings, pains, and death, will appear formidable even to the experienced Christian; but in the hope to glorify God, to leave a sinful world, and to be present with his Lord, he becomes ready to obey the Redeemer's call, and to follow Him through death to glory. It is the will of Christ that his disciples should mind their own duty, and not be curious about future events, either as to themselves or others. **Many things we are apt to be anxious about, which are nothing to us. Other people's affairs are nothing to us, to intermeddle in; we must quietly work, and mind our own business.** Many curious questions are put about the counsels of God, and the state of the unseen world, as to which we may say, **WHAT IS THIS TO US?** And if we attend to the duty of following Christ, we shall find neither heart nor time to meddle with that which does not belong to us. How little are any unwritten traditions to be relied upon! Let the Scripture be its own interpreter, and explain itself; as it is, in a great measure, its own evidence, and proves itself, for it is light. See the easy setting right such mistakes by the word of Christ. Scripture language is the safest channel for Scripture truth; the words which the Holy Ghost teaches, 1Co. 2:13 . Those who cannot agree in the same terms of art, and the application of them, may yet agree in the same Scripture terms, and to love one another.

Verse 25 Only a small part of the actions of Jesus had been written. But let us bless God for all that is in the Scriptures, and be thankful that there is so much in so small a space. Enough is recorded to direct our faith, and regulate our practice; more would have been unnecessary. Much of what is written is overlooked, much forgotten, and much made the matter of doubtful disputes. We may, however, look forward to the joy we shall receive in heaven, from a more complete knowledge of all Jesus did and said, as well as of the conduct of his providence and grace in his dealings with each of us. May this be our happiness. These are written that ye might believe that Jesus is the Christ, the Son of God; and that believing ye might have life through his name, ch. 20:31 .

REVELATION 13:18

Bible Versions Revelation 13:18 Compare Translations

Compare Translations for Revelation 13:18

Revelation 13:18 ASV

American Standard Version

Here is wisdom. He that hath understanding, let him count the number of the beast; for it is the number of a man: and his number is Six hundred and sixty and six.

Revelation 13:18 BBE

Bible in Basic English

Here is wisdom. He who has knowledge let him get the number of the beast; because it is the number of a man: and his number is Six hundred and sixty-six.

Revelation 13:18 CEB

Common English Bible

This calls for wisdom. Let the one who understands calculate the beast's number, for it's a human being's number. Its number is six hundred sixty-six.

Revelation 13:18 CJB

Complete Jewish Bible < NOTE: Added as follows -

Complete Jewish Bible, CJB
The Complete Jewish Bible is the only English version of the Bible fully Jewish in style and presentation that includes both the Tanakh ("Old Testament") and the B'rit Hadashah (New Covenant, "New Testament"). Even its title, the Complete Jewish Bible, challenges both Jews and Christians to see that the whole Bible is Jewish, the B'rit Hadashah as well as the Tanakh. Jews are challenged by the implication that without it the Tanakh is an incomplete Bible. Christians are challenged with the fact that they are joined to the Jewish people through faith in the Jewish Messiah, Yeshua (Jesus) -- so that because Christianity can be rightly understood only from a Jewish perspective, anti-Semitism is condemned absolutely and forever. In short, the Complete Jewish Bible restores the Jewish unity of the Bible. Also for the first time the information needed for the synagogue readings from the Torah and the Prophets is completely integrated with similar use of the B'rit Hadashah. You can get more information on this unique Bible version at http://www.messianicjewish.net/jntp/complete-jewish-bible.html.

FRANK M. CONAWAY, JR.

About the Translator

David H. Stern was born in Los Angeles in 1935, the great-grandson of two of the city's first twenty Jews. He earned a Ph.D. in economics at Princeton University and was a professor at UCLA, mountain-climber, co-author of a book on surfing, and owner of health-food stores.

In 1972, he came to believe in Yeshua as the Messiah, after which he received a Master of Divinity degree at Fuller Theological Seminary and did graduate work at the University of Judaism. Dr. Stern taught Fuller Theological Seminary's first course in "Judaism and Christianity," organized Messianic Jewish conferences and leaders' meetings, and was an officer of the Messianic Jewish Alliance of America.

Dr. Stern is the author of Messianic Jewish Manifesto, which outlines the destiny, identity, history, theology and program of today's Messianic Jewish movement. He also wrote Restoring the Jewishness of the Gospel: A Message for Christians. It consists of excerpts from the former book selected for Christians to whom the Jewishness of the Gospel is an unfamiliar idea.

His Jewish New Testament, which has been incorporated into the Complete Jewish Bible, is the basis for its companion volume, the Jewish New Testament Commentary. This book discusses Jewish issues raised in the New Testament -- questions Jews have about Yeshua, the New Testament and Christianity; questions Christians have about Judaism and the Jewish roots of their faith; and questions Messianic Jews have about their own identity and role. >

This is where wisdom is needed; those who understand should count the number of the beast, for it is the number of a person, and its number is 666.

Revelation 13:18 RHE

Douay-Rheims

Here is wisdom. He that hath understanding, let him count the number of the beast. For it is the number of a man: and the number of him is six hundred sixty-six.

Revelation 13:18 ESV

English Standard Version

This calls for wisdom: let the one who has understanding calculate the number of the beast, for it is the number of a man, and his number is 666.

Revelation 13:18 GW

GOD'S WORD Translation

In this situation wisdom is needed. Let the person who has insight figure out the number of the beast, because it is a human number. The beast's number is 666.

INTELLIGENT REVELATION

< I had to break in here because I seem to like this version best. I found it in The Good News Bible - Today's English Version. It seems that at one time it was used by Father Damien who was a Catholic Chaplain at The Baltimore City Jail. It is just something about the way that it is put that makes me feel a certain way inside! >

Revelation 13:18 GNT

Good News Translation

This calls for wisdom. Whoever is intelligent can figure out the meaning of the number of the beast, because the number stands for the name of someone. Its number is 666.

Revelation 13:18 HNV

Hebrew Names Version

Here is wisdom. He who has understanding, let him calculate the number of the beast, for it is the number of a man. His number is six hundred sixty-six.

Revelation 13:18 CSB

Holman Christian Standard

Here is wisdom: The one who has understanding must calculate the number of the beast, because it is the number of a man. His number is 666.

Revelation 13:18 KJV

King James Version

Here is wisdom. Let him that hath understanding count the number of the beast: for it is the number of a man; and his number is Six hundred threescore and six.

Revelation 13:18 LEB

Lexham English Bible

Here is wisdom: the one who has understanding, let him calculate the number of the beast, for it is man's number, and his number [is] six hundred sixty-six.

Revelation 13:18 NAS

New American Standard

Here is wisdom. Let him who has understanding calculate the number of the beast, for the number is that of a man ; and his number is six hundred and sixty-six .

Revelation 13:18 NCV

New Century Version

This takes wisdom. Let the one who has understanding find the meaning of the number, which is the number of a person. Its number is six hundred sixty-six.

Revelation 13:18 NIRV

New International Reader's Version

Here is a problem that you have to be wise to figure out. If you can, figure out what the beast's number means. It is man's number. His number is 666.

Revelation 13:18 NIV

New International Version

This calls for wisdom. If anyone has insight, let him calculate the number of the beast, for it is man's number. His number is 666.

Revelation 13:18 NKJV

New King James Version

Here is wisdom. Let him who has understanding calculate the number of the beast, for it is the number of a man: His number is 666.

Revelation 13:18 NLT

New Living Translation

Wisdom is needed to understand this. Let the one who has understanding solve the number of the beast, for it is the number of a man. His number is 666.

Revelation 13:18 NRS

New Revised Standard

This calls for wisdom: let anyone with understanding calculate the number of the beast, for it is the number of a person. Its number is six hundred sixty-six.

Revelation 13:18 RSV

Revised Standard Version

This calls for wisdom: let him who has understanding reckon the number of the beast, for it is a human number, its number is six hundred and sixty-six.

Revelation 13:18 DBY

The Darby Translation

Here is wisdom. He that has understanding let him count the number of the beast: for it is a man's number; and its number [is] six hundred [and] sixty-six.

Revelation 13:18 MSG

The Message

Solve a riddle: Put your heads together and figure out the meaning of the number of the Beast. It's a human number: six hundred sixty-six.

Revelation 13:18 WBT

The Webster Bible

Here is wisdom. Let him that hath understanding count the number of the beast: for it is the number of a man; and his number [is] six hundred and sixty six.

Revelation 13:18 TMB

Third Millennium Bible

Here is wisdom: Let him that hath understanding count the number of the beast, for it is the number of a man; and his number is six hundred threescore and six.

Revelation 13:18 TNIV

Today's New International Version

This calls for wisdom. Let those who have insight calculate the number of the beast, for it is the number of a man. That number is 666.

Revelation 13:18 TYN

Tyndale

Here is wisdom. Let him that hath wytt count the nombre of the beest. For it is the nombre of a man and his nombre is sixe hondred threscore and sixe.

Revelation 13:18 WNT

Weymouth New Testament

Here is scope for ingenuity. Let people of shrewd intelligence calculate the number of the Wild Beast; for it indicates a certain man, and his number is 666.

Revelation 13:18 WEB

World English Bible

Here is wisdom. He who has understanding, let him calculate the number of the beast, for it is the number of a man. His number is six hundred sixty-six.

Revelation 13:18 WYC

Wycliffe

Here is wisdom; he that hath understanding, account the number of the beast; for it is the number of man, and his number is six hundred sixty and six.

Revelation 13:18 YLT

Young's Literal Translation

Here is the wisdom! He who is having the understanding, let him count the number of the beast, for the number of a man it is, and its number [is] 666.

Revelation 13 Commentary - Matthew Henry Commentary on the Whole Bible (Concise)

Chapter 13

A wild beast rises out of the sea, to whom the dragon gives his power. (1-10) Another beast, which has two horns like a lamb, but speaks as a dragon. (11-15) It obliges all to worship its image, and receive its mark, as persons devoted to it. (16-18)

Verses 1-10 The apostle, standing on the shore, saw a savage beast rise out of the sea; a tyrannical, idolatrous, persecuting power, springing up out of the troubles which took place. It was a frightful monster! It appears to mean that worldly, oppressing dominion, which for many ages, even from the times of the Babylonish captivity, had been hostile to the church. The first beast then began to oppress and persecute the righteous for righteousness' sake, but they suffered most under the fourth beast of Daniel, (the Roman empire,) which has afflicted the saints with many cruel persecutions. The source of its power was the dragon. It was set up by the devil, and supported by him. The wounding the head may be the abolishing pagan idolatry; and the healing of the wound, introducing popish idolatry, the same in substance, only in a new dress, but which as effectually answers the devil's design. The world admired its power, policy and success. They paid honor and subjection to the devil and his instruments. It exercised infernal power and policy, requiring men to render that honor to creatures which belongs to God alone. Yet the devil's power and success are limited. Christ has a chosen remnant, redeemed by his blood, recorded in his book, sealed by his Spirit; and though the devil and antichrist may overcome the body, and take away the natural life, they cannot conquer the soul, nor prevail with true believers to forsake their Saviour, and join his enemies. Perseverance in the faith of the gospel and true worship of God, in this great hour of trial and temptation, which would deceive all but the elect, is the character of those registered in the book of life. This powerful motive and encouragement to constancy, is the great design of the whole Revelation.

Verses 11-18 Those who understand the first beast to denote a worldly power, take the second to be also a persecuting and assumed power, which acts under the disguise of religion, and of charity to the souls of men. It is a spiritual dominion, professing to be derived from Christ, and exercised at first in a gentle manner, but soon spake like the dragon. Its speech betrayed it; for it gives forth those false doctrines and cruel decrees, which show it to belong to the dragon, and not to the Lamb. It exercised all the power of the former beast. It pursues the same design, to draw men from worshipping the true God, and to subject the souls of men to the will and control of men. The second beast has carried on its designs, by methods whereby men should be deceived to worship the former beast, in the new shape, or likeness made for it. By lying wonders, pretended miracles. And by severe censures. Also by allowing none to enjoy natural or civil rights, who will not worship that beast which is the image of the pagan beast. It is made a qualification for buying and selling, as well as for places of profit and trust, that they oblige themselves to use all their interest, power, and **endeavour,** to forward the dominion of the beast, which is meant by receiving his mark. To make an image to the beast, whose deadly wound was healed, would be to give form and power to his worship, or to require obedience to his commands. To worship the image of the beast, implies being subject to those things which stamp the character of the picture, and render it the image of the beast. The number of the beast is given, so as to show the infinite wisdom of God, and to exercise the wisdom of men. **The number is the number of a man, computed after the usual manner among men, and it is 666. What or who is intended by this, remains a mystery < FMCJR: NOT TO ME >.** To almost every religious dispute this number has yet been applied, and it may reasonably be doubted whether the meaning has yet been discovered. But he who has wisdom and understanding, will see that all the enemies of God are numbered and marked out for destruction; that the term of their power will soon expire, and that all nations shall submit to our King of righteousness and peace.

Revelation 13 Commentary - Commentary Critical and Explanatory on the Whole Bible

CHAPTER 13

FRANK M. CONAWAY, JR.

Revelation 13:1-18 . VISION OF THE BEAST THAT CAME OUT OF THE SEA: THE
SECOND BEAST, OUT OF THE EARTH, EXERCISING THE POWER OF THE FIRST
BEAST, AND CAUSING THE EARTH TO WORSHIP HIM.

1. I stood--So B, Aleph, and Coptic read. But A, C, Vulgate, and Syriac, "He stood." Standing on
the sand of the sea, HE gave his power to the beast that rose out of the sea.
upon the sand of the sea--where the four winds were to be seen striving upon the great sea (
Daniel 7:2).
beast--Greek, "wild beast." Man becomes "brutish" when he severs himself from God, the
archetype and true ideal, in whose image he was first made, which ideal is realized by the man
Christ Jesus. Hence, the world powers seeking their own glory, and not God's, are represented as
beasts; and Nebuchadnezzar, when in self-deification he forgot that "the Most High ruleth in the
kingdom of men," was driven among the beasts. In Daniel 7:4-7 there are four beasts: here the
one beast expresses the sum-total of the God-opposed world power viewed in its universal
development, not restricted to one manifestation alone, as Rome. This first beast expresses the
world power attacking the Church more from without; the second, which is a revival of, and
minister to, the first, is the world power as the false prophet corrupting and destroying the
Church from within.
out of the sea--(Daniel 7:3 ; compare Note, peoples, multitudes, nations, and tongues. The earth
(Revelation 13:11), on the other hand, means the consolidated, ordered world of nations, with
its culture and learning.
seven heads and ten horns--A, B, and C transpose, "ten horns and seven heads." The ten horns
are now put first (contrast the order, Revelation 12:3) because they are crowned. They shall not
be so till the last stage of the fourth kingdom (the Roman), which shall continue until the fifth
kingdom, Christ's, shall supplant it and destroy it utterly; this last stage is marked by the ten toes
of the two feet of the image in Daniel 2:33Daniel 2:41Daniel 2:42 . The seven implies the world
power setting up itself as God, and caricaturing the seven Spirits of God; yet its true character as
God-opposed is detected by the number ten accompanying the seven. Dragon and beast both
wear crowns, but the former on the heads, the latter on the horns (Revelation 12:3 , 13:1).
Therefore, both heads and horns refer to kingdoms; compare Revelation 17:7Revelation
17:10Revelation 17:12 , "kings" representing the kingdoms whose heads they are. The seven
kings, as peculiarly powerful--the great powers of the world--are distinguished from the ten,
represented by the horns (simply called "kings," Revelation 17:12). In Daniel, the ten mean the
last phase of the world power, the fourth kingdom divided into ten parts. They are connected
with the seventh head (Revelation 17:12), and are as yet future [AUBERLEN]. The mistake of
those who interpret the beast to be Rome exclusively, and the ten horns to mean kingdoms which
have taken the place of Rome in Europe already, is, the fourth kingdom in the image has TWO
legs, representing the eastern as well as the western empire; the ten toes are not upon the one foot
(the west), as these interpretations require, but on the two (east and west) together, so that any
theory which makes the ten kingdoms belong to the west alone must err. If the ten kingdoms
meant were those which sprung up on the overthrow of Rome, the ten would be accurately

known, whereas twenty-eight different lists are given by so many interpreters, making in all sixty-five kingdoms! [TYSO in DE BURGH]. The seven heads are the seven world monarchies, Egypt, Assyria, Babylon, Persia, Greece, Rome, the Germanic empire, under the last of which we live [AUBERLEN], and which devolved for a time on Napoleon, after Francis, emperor of Germany and king of Rome, had resigned the title in 1806. FABER explains the healing of the deadly wound to be the revival of the Napoleonic dynasty after its overthrow at Waterloo. That secular dynasty, in alliance with the ecclesiastical power, the Papacy (Revelation 13:11 , &c.), being "the eighth head," and yet "of the seven" (Revelation 17:11), will temporarily triumph over the saints, until destroyed in Armageddon (Revelation 19:17-21). A Napoleon, in this view, will be the Antichrist, restoring the Jews to Palestine, and accepted as their Messiah at first, and afterwards fearfully oppressing them. Antichrist, the summing up and concentration of all the world evil that preceded, is the eighth, but yet one of the seven (Revelation 17:11). crowns--Greek, "diadems."

name of blasphemy--So C, Coptic, and ANDREAS. A, B, and Vulgate read, "names of blasphemy," namely, a name on each of the heads; blasphemously arrogating attributes belonging to God alone (compare Note, little horn in Daniel 7:8Daniel 7:20Daniel 7:21 , 2 Thessalonians 2:4 .

2. leopard . . . bear . . . lion--This beast unites in itself the God-opposed characteristics of the three preceding kingdoms, resembling respectively the leopard, bear, and lion. It rises up out of the sea, as Daniel's four beasts, and has ten horns, as Daniel's fourth beast, and seven heads, as Daniel's four beasts had in all, namely, one on the first, one on the second, four on the third, and one on the fourth. Thus it represents comprehensively in one figure the world power (which in Daniel is represented by four) of all times and places, not merely of one period and one locality, viewed as opposed to God; just as the woman is the Church of all ages. This view is favored also by the fact, that the beast is the vicarious representative of Satan, who similarly has seven heads and ten horns: a general description of his universal power in all ages and places of the world. Satan appears as a serpent, as being the archetype of the beast nature (Revelation 12:9). "If the seven heads meant merely seven Roman emperors, one cannot understand why they alone should be mentioned in the original image of Satan, whereas it is perfectly intelligible if we suppose them to represent Satan's power on earth viewed collectively" [AUBERLEN].

3. One of--literally, "from among."
wounded . . . healed--twice again repeated emphatically (Revelation 13:12Revelation 13:14); compare Revelation 17:8Revelation 17:11 , "the beast that was, and is not, and shall ascend out of the bottomless pit" (compare Revelation 13:11); the Germanic empire, the seventh head (revived in the eighth), as yet future in John's time (Revelation 17:10). Contrast the change whereby Nebuchadnezzar, being humbled from his self-deifying pride, was converted from his beast-like form and character to MAN'S form and true position towards God; symbolized by his eagle wings being plucked, and himself made to stand upon his feet as a man (Daniel 7:4). Here, on the contrary, the beast's head is not changed into a human head, but receives a deadly

wound, that is, the world kingdom which this head represents does not truly turn to God, but for a time its God-opposed character remains paralyzed ("as it were slain"; the very words marking the beast's outward resemblance to the Lamb, "as it were slain," second beast's resemblance to the Lamb,Revelation 13:11). Though seemingly slain (Greek for "wounded"), it remains the beast still, to rise again in another form (Revelation 13:11). The first six heads were heathenish, Egypt, Assyria, Babylon, Persia, Greece, Rome; the new seventh world power (the pagan German hordes pouring down on Christianized Rome), whereby Satan had hoped to stifle Christianity (Revelation 11:15Revelation 11:16), became itself Christianized (answering to the beast's, as it were, deadly wound: it was slain, and it is not,Revelation 17:11). Its ascent out of the bottomless pit answers to the healing of its deadly wound (Revelation 17:8). No essential change is noticed in Daniel as effected by Christianity upon the fourth kingdom; it remains essentially God-opposed to the last. The beast, healed of its temporary and external wound, now returns, not only from the sea, but from the bottomless pit, whence it draws new Antichristian strength of hell (Revelation 13:3Revelation 13:11Revelation 13:12Revelation 13:14 , Revelation 11:7 , 17:8). Compare the seven evil spirits taken into the temporarily dispossessed, and the last state worse than the first,Matthew 12:43-45 . A new and worse heathenism breaks in upon the Christianized world, more devilish than the old one of the first heads of the beast. The latter was an apostasy only from the general revelation of God in nature and conscience; but this new one is from God's revelation of love in His Son. It culminates in Antichrist, the man of sin, the son of perdition (compare Revelation 17:11); 2 Thessalonians 2:3 ; compare 2 Timothy 3:1-4 , the very characteristics of old heathenism (Romans 1:29-32) [AUBERLEN]. More than one wound seems to me to be meant, for example, that under Constantine (when the pagan worship of the emperor's image gave way to Christianity), followed by the healing, when image worship and the other papal errors were introduced into the Church; again, that at the Reformation, followed by the lethargic form of godliness without the power, and about to end in the last great apostasy, which I identify with the second beast (Revelation 13:11), Antichrist, the same seventh world power in another form.
wondered after--followed with wondering gaze.

4. which gave--A, B, C, Vulgate, Syriac, and ANDREAS read, "because he gave."
power--Greek, "the authority" which it had; its authority.
Who is like unto the beast?--The very language appropriated to God,Exodus 15:11 (whence, in the Hebrew, the Maccabees took their name; the opponents of the Old Testament Antichrist, Antiochus); Psalms 35:10 , 71:19 , 113:5 , Micah 7:18 ; blasphemously (Revelation 13:1Revelation 13:5) assigned to the beast. It is a parody of the name "Michael" (compare Revelation 12:7), meaning, "Who is like unto God?"

5. blasphemies--So ANDREAS reads. B reads "blasphemy." A, "blasphemous things" (compare Daniel 7:8 , 11:25).
power--"authority"; legitimate power (Greek, "exousia").
to continue--Greek, "poiesai," "to act," or "work." B reads, "to make war" (compare Revelation

13:4). But A, C, Vulgate, Syriac, and ANDREAS omit "war."
forty . . . two

6. opened . . . mouth--The usual formula in the case of a set speech, or series of speeches.
Revelation 13:6Revelation 13:7 expand Revelation 13:5 .
blasphemy--So B and ANDREAS. A and C read "blasphemies."
and them--So Vulgate, Coptic, ANDREAS, and PRIMASIUS read. A and C omit "and": "them
that dwell (literally, 'tabernacle') in heaven," mean not only angels and the departed souls of the
righteous, but believers on earth who have their citizenship in heaven, and whose true life is
hidden from the Antichristian persecutor in the secret of God's tabernacle.

7. power--Greek, "authority."
all kindreds . . . tongues . . . nations--Greek, "every tribe . . . tongue . . . nation." A, B, C,
Vulgate, Syriac, ANDREAS, and PRIMASIUS add "and people," after "tribe" or "kindred."

8. all that dwell upon the earth--being of earth earthy; in contrast to "them that dwell in heaven."
whose names are not written--A, B, C, Syriac, Coptic, and ANDREAS read singular, "(every
one) whose (Greek, 'hou'; but B, Greek, 'hon,' plural) name is not written."
Lamb slain from the foundation of the world--The Greek order of words favors this translation.
He was slain in the Father's eternal counsels: compare 1 Peter 1:191 Peter 1:20 , virtually
parallel. The other way of connecting the words is, "Written from the foundation of the world in
the book of life of the Lamb slain." So in Revelation 17:8 . The elect. The former is in the Greek
more obvious and simple. "Whatsoever virtue was in the sacrifices, did operate through
Messiah's death alone. As He was "the Lamb slain from the foundation of the world," so all
atonements ever made were only effectual by His blood" [BISHOP PEARSON, Exposition of
the Creed].

9. A general exhortation. Christ's own words of monition calling solemn attention.

10. He that leadeth into captivity--A, B, C, and Vulgate read, "if any one (be) for captivity."
shall go into captivity--Greek present, "goeth into captivity." Compare Jeremiah 15:2 , which is
alluded to here. Aleph, B, and C read simply, "he goeth away," and omit "into captivity." But A
and Vulgate support the words.
he that killeth with the sword, must be killed with the sword--So B and C read. But A reads, "if
any (is for) being (literally, 'to be') killed with the sword." As of old, so now, those to be
persecuted by the beast in various ways, have their trials severally appointed them by God's fixed
counsel. English Version is quite a different sense, namely, a warning to the persecutors that they
shall be punished with retribution in kind.
Here--"Herein": in bearing their appointed sufferings lies the patient endurance . . . of the saints.
This is to be the motto and watchword of the elect during the period of the world kingdom. As
the first beast is to be met by patience and faith (Revelation 13:10), the second beast must be
opposed by true wisdom (Revelation 13:18).

11. another beast--"the false prophet."

out of the earth--out of society civilized, consolidated, and ordered, but still, with all its culture, of earth earthy: as distinguished from "the sea," the troubled agitations of various peoples out of which the world power and its several kingdoms have emerged. "The sacerdotal persecuting power, pagan and Christian; the pagan priesthood making an image of the emperors which they compelled Christians to worship, and working wonders by magic and omens; the Romish priesthood, the inheritors of pagan rites, images, and superstitions, lamb-like in Christian professions, dragon-like in word and act" [ALFORD, and so the Spanish Jesuit, LACUNZA, writing under the name BEN EZRA]. As the first beast was like the Lamb in being, as it were, wounded to death, so the second is like the Lamb in having two lamb-like horns (**its** essential difference from the Lamb is marked by its having TWO, but the Lamb SEVEN horns, Revelation 5:6). The former paganism of the world power, seeming to be wounded to death by Christianity, revives. In its second beast-form it is Christianized heathendom ministering to the former, and having earthly culture and learning to recommend it. The second beast's, or false prophet's rise, coincides in time with the healing of the beast's deadly wound and its revival (Revelation 13:12-14). Its manifold character is marked by the Lord (Matthew 24:11Matthew 24:24), "Many false prophets shall rise," where He is speaking of the last days. As the former beast corresponds to the first four beasts of Daniel, so the second beast, or the false prophet, to the little horn starting up among the ten horns of the fourth beast. This Antichristian horn has not only the mouth of blasphemy (Revelation 13:5), but also "the eyes of man" (Daniel 7:8): the former is also in the first beast (Revelation 13:1Revelation 13:5), but the latter not so. "The eyes of man" symbolize cunning and intellectual culture, the very characteristic of "the false prophet" (Revelation 13:13-15 , Revelation 16:14). The first beast is physical and political; the second a spiritual power, the power of knowledge, ideas (the favorite term in the French school of politics), and scientific cultivation. Both alike are beasts, from below, not from above; faithful allies, worldly Antichristian wisdom standing in the service of the worldly Antichristian power: the dragon is both lion and serpent: might and cunning are his armory. The dragon gives his external power to the first beast (Revelation 13:2), his spirit to the second, so that it speaks as a dragon (Revelation 13:11). The second, arising out of the earth, is in Revelation 11:7 , 17:8 , said to ascend out of the bottomless pit: **its** very culture and world wisdom only intensify its infernal character, the pretense to superior knowledge and rationalistic philosophy (as in the primeval temptation, Genesis 3:5Genesis 3:7 , "their EYES [as here] were opened") veiling the deification of nature, self, and man. Hence spring Idealism, Materialism, Deism, Pantheism, Atheism. Antichrist shall be the culmination. The Papacy's claim to the double power, secular and spiritual, is a sample and type of the twofold beast, that out of the sea, and that out of the earth, or bottomless pit. Antichrist will be the climax, and final form. PRIMASIUS OF ADRUMENTUM, in the sixth century, says, "He feigns to be a lamb that he may assail the Lamb--the body of Christ."

12. power--Greek, "authority."

before him--"in his presence"; as ministering to, and upholding him. "The non-existence of the

---

beast embraces the whole Germanic Christian period. The healing of the wound and return of the beast is represented [in regard to its final Antichristian manifestation though including also, meanwhile, its healing and return under Popery, which is baptized heathenism] in that principle which, since 1789, has manifested itself in beast-like outbreaks" [AUBERLEN].
which dwell therein--the earthly-minded. The Church becomes the harlot: the world's political power, the Antichristian beast; the world's wisdom and civilization, the false prophet. Christ's three offices are thus perverted: the first beast is the false kingship; the harlot, the false priesthood; the second beast, the false prophet. The beast is the bodily, the false prophet the intellectual, the harlot the spiritual power of Antichristianity [AUBERLEN]. The Old-Testament Church stood under the power of the beast, the heathen world power: the Middle-Ages Church under that of the harlot: in modern times the false prophet predominates. But in the last days all these God-opposed powers which have succeeded each other shall co-operate, and raise each other to the most terrible and intense power of their nature: the false prophet causes men to worship the beast, and the beast carries the harlot. These three forms of apostasy are reducible to two: the apostate Church and the apostate world, pseudo-Christianity and Antichristianity, the harlot and the beast; for the false prophet is also a beast; and the two beasts, as different manifestations of the same beast-like principle, stand in contradistinction to the harlot, and are finally judged together, whereas separate judgment falls on the harlot [AUBERLEN].
deadly wound--Greek, "wound of death."

13. wonders--Greek, "signs."
so that--so great that.
maketh fire--Greek, "maketh even fire." This is the very miracle which the two witnesses perform, and which Elijah long ago had performed; this the beast from the bottomless pit, or the false prophet, mimics. Not merely tricks, but miracles of a demoniacal kind, and by demon aid, like those of the Egyptian magicians, shall be wrought, most calculated to deceive; wrought "after the working (Greek, 'energy') of Satan."

14. deceiveth them that dwell on the earth--the earthly-minded, but not the elect. Even a miracle is not enough to warrant belief in a professed revelation unless that revelation be in harmony with God's already revealed will.
by the means of those miracles--rather as Greek, "on account of (because of; in consequence of) those miracles."
which he had power to do--Greek, "which were given him to do."
in the sight of the beast--"before him" (Revelation 13:12).
which--A, B, and C read, "who"; marking, perhaps, a personal Antichrist.
had--So B and ANDREAS read. But A, C, and Vulgate read, "hath."

15. he had power--Greek, "it was given to him."
to give life--Greek, "breath," or "spirit."
image--Nebuchadnezzar set up in Dura a golden image to be worshipped, probably of himself;

for his dream had been interpreted, "Thou art this head of gold"; the three Hebrews who refused to worship the image were east into a burning furnace. All this typifies the last apostasy. PLINY, in his letter to Trajan, states that he consigned to punishment those Christians who would not worship the emperor's image with incense and wine. So JULIAN, the apostate, set up his own image with the idols of the heathen gods in the Forum, that the Christians in doing reverence to it, might seem to worship the idols. So Charlemagne's image was set up for homage; and the Pope adored the new emperor [DUPIN, vol. 6, p. 126]. Napoleon, the successor of Charlemagne, designed after he had first lowered the Pope by removing him to Fontainebleau, then to "make an idol of him" [Memorial de Sainte Helene]; keeping the Pope near him, he would, through the Pope's influence, have directed the religious, as well as the political world. The revived Napoleonic dynasty may, in some one representative, realize the project, becoming the beast supported by the false prophet (perhaps some openly infidel supplanter of the papacy, under a spiritual guise, after the harlot, or apostate Church, who is distinct from the second beast, has been stripped and judged by the beast, Revelation 17:16); he then might have an image set up in his honor as a test of secular and spiritual allegiance.

speak--"False doctrine will give a spiritual, philosophical appearance to the foolish apotheosis of the creaturely personified by Antichrist" [AUBERLEN]. JEROME, on Daniel 7, says, Antichrist shall be "one of the human race in whom the whole of Satan shall dwell bodily." Rome's speaking images and winking pictures of the Virgin Mary and the saints are an earnest of the future demoniacal miracles of the false prophet in making the beast's or Antichrist's image to speak.

16. to receive a mark--literally, "that they should give them a mark"; such a brand as masters stamp on their slaves, and monarchs on their subjects. Soldiers voluntarily punctured their arms with marks of the general under whom they served. Votaries of idols branded themselves with the idol's cipher or symbol. Thus Antiochus Epiphanes branded the Jews with the ivy leaf, the symbol of Bacchus (2 Maccabees 6:7; 3 Maccabees 2:29). Contrast God's seal and name in the foreheads of His servants,Revelation 7:3 , 14:1 , 22:4 ; and Galatians 6:17 , "I bear in my body the marks of the Lord Jesus," that is, I am His soldier and servant. The mark in the right hand and forehead implies the prostration of bodily and intellectual powers to the beast's domination. "In the forehead by way of profession; in the hand with respect to work and service" [AUGUSTINE].

17. And--So A, B, and Vulgate read. C, IRENAEUS, 316, Coptic, and Syriac omit it.
might buy--Greek, "may be able to buy."
the mark, or the name--Greek, "the mark (namely), the name of the beast." The mark may be, as in the case of the sealing of the saints in the forehead, not a visible mark, but symbolical of allegiance. So the sign of the cross in Popery. The Pope's interdict has often shut out the excommunicate from social and commercial intercourse. Under the final Antichrist this shall come to pass in its most violent form.
number of his name--implying that the name has some numerical meaning.

18. wisdom--the armory against the second beast, as patience and faith against the first. Spiritual wisdom is needed to solve the mystery of iniquity, so as not to be beguiled by it.

count . . . for--The "for" implies the possibility of our calculating or counting the beast's number. the number of a man--that is, counted as men generally count. So the phrase is used in Revelation 21:17 . The number is the number of a man, not of God; he shall extol himself above the power of the Godhead, as the MAN of sin [AQUINAS]. Though it is an imitation of the divine name, it is only human.

six hundred threescore and six--A and Vulgate write the numbers in full in the Greek. But B writes merely the three Greek letters standing for numbers, Ch, X, St. "C reads" 616, but IRENAEUS, 328, opposes this and maintains "666." IRENAEUS, in the second century, disciple of POLYCARP, John's disciple, explained this number as contained in the Greek letters of Lateinos (L being thirty; A, one; T, three hundred; E, five; I, ten; N, fifty; O, seventy; S, two hundred). The Latin is peculiarly the language of the Church of Rome in all her official acts; the forced unity of language in ritual being the counterfeit of the true unity; the premature and spurious anticipation of the real unity, only to be realized at Christ's coming, when all the earth shall speak "one language" (Zephaniah 3:9). The last Antichrist may have a close connection with Rome, and so the name Lateinos (666) may apply to him. The Hebrew letters of Balaam amount to 666 [BUNSEN]; a type of the false prophet, whose characteristic, like Balaam's, will be high spiritual knowledge perverted to Satanic ends. The number six is the world number; in 666 it occurs in units, tens, and hundreds. It is next neighbor to the sacred seven, but is severed from it by an impassable gulf. It is the number of the world given over to judgment; hence there is a pause between the sixth and seventh seals, and the sixth and seventh trumpets. The judgments on the world are complete in six; by the fulfilment of seven, the kingdoms of the world become Christ's. As twelve is the number of the Church, so six, its half, symbolizes the world kingdom broken. The raising of the six to **tens** and hundreds (higher powers) indicates that **the beast**, notwithstanding his progression to higher powers, can only rise to greater ripeness for judgment. Thus 666, the judged world power, contrasts with the 144,000 sealed and transfigured ones (the Church number, twelve, squared and multiplied by one thousand, the number symbolizing the world pervaded by God; ten, the world number, raised to the power of three the number of God) [AUBERLEN]. The "mark" (Greek, "**charagma**") and "name" are one and the same. The first two radical letters of Christ (Greek, "**Christos**"), Ch and R, are the same as the first two of charagma, and were the imperial monogram of Christian Rome. Antichrist, personating Christ, adopts a symbol like, but not agreeing with, Christ's monogram, Ch, X, St; whereas the radicals in "Christ" are Ch, R, St. Papal Rome has similarly substituted the standard of the Keys for the standard of the Cross; so on the papal coinage (the image of power, Matthew 22:20). The two first letters of "Christ," Ch, R, represent seven hundred, the perfect number. The Ch, X, St represent an imperfect number, a triple falling away (apostasy) from septenary perfection [WORDSWORTH].

IS NOT KUNDALINI

KUNDALINI CALL OUT

THE LAST KUNDALINI MASTER

I feel the need to write this like this because I feel that so much has and is being written about the subject called kundalini. What is kundalini? I feel that this should be answered. It seems kind of simple to me now. A person could have the "full" kundalini experience and not know what it was. That happened to me. I had done it, but did not know what I had done! What had I done? I had done the " Kundalini Thing ". And what does the " Kundalini Thing " do exactly? Right! I now feel that there are a lot of people writing about the subject based upon old writings and adding scientific wild ass guess to the ancient concepts. In high school physics we called this SWAG. This was used in a multiple choice test where the answer was not known. First you rule out the answers that you do not think are correct, then you make your best guess.

ELEMENTS OF KUNDALINI

You are not talking about kundalini opening unless you at least talk about these things:

The three "ductless glands" of kundalini called ida, pangala, and shushmna.

The "two ductless glands" in the sides of the jaws called ida and pangala.

The hole in the roof of the mouth that draws the fluid of shushmna which is the spine.

The "mystic" coma or **orifice locks**, which is to perform all the yogi body posture locks at the same time.

The Sphinx pose or posture.

How do you breath when you enter the house of terror called the mystic coma?

It should be noted that the mystic coma or house of terror is The Sphinx.

The Sphinx means father of terror. It is the body or animal self buried in a grave with the spiritual self of head extending into the world. Hence to be buried in a shallow < s – hallow > grave.

The mystic tones of the kundalini coil opening caused by the internal sounds of the fluids moving and the **binaural** beat induction produced in the brain and cranial cavity.

The neck lock causing great pressure on the teeth to the point that they may feel plastic like to activate the related nerves in the spine.

The electro-magnetic stimulation of the different brain centers as shown in art work as rays of light extending from the different areas of the head leading to the automatic body motions called postures.

The drawing of the waters of life from the sun and the moon, which is ida and pangala drawing the fluids of life from the testes.

The root seal which is the prostrate < pump > closes or contracts as **sushumna** < be quiet and calm man - sushumna > is loaded with a bulbs worth of fluid pushing upward towards the neck lock. This is called to reverse the pole. When the spine is fully loaded and the student begins to draw upon the fluids of ida and pangala thru the mouth, that is called to reverse the < three > poles < or to raise the pitched fork > . The ureaus symbol or your ray < of light > of Ra and Isis happened at the crossing point inside the head behind the forehead. The rear path is that of the spine and the front path is that of the fluid that comes from the two jaw side glandless ducts and the roof of the mouth valve, which is from the base of the skull. This valve, so to speak, when opened releases the mouth / teeth lock pressure; thereby causing the neck gate or lock to open. The sound of terrible wind rushing thru a large tunnel announcing a **huge** body of liquid behind it. The fluid is not only being moved by the pushing upward pressure from below, but the negative drawing upward pressure or **vacuum** from below the neck lock. Think of a fluid train or pellet moving up the spine into voids of pressure, also being assisted by the brain using the spine like a tail or vertical drawing pump. This also helps cause the swirling or upward spinning motion of the fluid. It is the **swirling** inner motion that martial artists see with the inner meditative eye

DRAWING KUNG

What is " drawing kung "? Drawing kung is a way to reverse pressurize the upper third gate of the body. The objective is to create a negative pressure in the upper third chamber of the body, while creating a positive pressure in the lower most chambers of the body. The **medulla oblongata** < oblongate > lock helps cause this as the Yogi uses the mouth seal method of drawing elixir.

" Drawing elixir " is to pressurize the " Hood of Ra ", or the mouth while pressurizing it by keeping the mouth sealed while drawing / drinking the nectar from Ida, Pingala, and Shushma. The lower gate, or pyramid begins to < by you **pulsing upon the prostate < prostrate > pump say** 200 times to prime the lower gate system while in the **medulla oblongate** lock – hence creating pressure upward above the lower pyramids which are called the sun, moon, and earth pyramids of the lower gate which are the prostrate pump < egg or oval sphere > and the greater and lesser spheres which are the testes. > **pulse.** It is as if the sun and moon are charging the earth lower chakra sphere via the pyramid < electro-magnetic liquid center of which the image in some yogi books show the " opening of the skull / skill >. Hence, the lower gate is of the positive pressure charge, and the upper head chamber is of an drawing negative pressure charge; therefore the central path < body / spine > can do nothing but draw the below " Chang " upwards into the path of the spine to confront the blockers or the opened gated path. Hence – Kundan < Kundalini > . As a note, one might think that life is linear, but it is not! There are levels and steps to that called life. You must move to get to the next level! Notice I did not give a direction or a move count.

ENOUGH

I had enough of all of this hard times, so I thought. I had already ciphered King Pakal's sarcophagus lid a year ago. Guess what, I can't find it. So as a result I had to cipher it again. I saw it on the History channels show called ANCIENT ALIENS: EARLY CIVILIZATIONS TO MODERN TIMES. When I saw the image I thought I knew what it was. It was very funny to hear the comments about the image. I said to myself that it looked like " the inner workings of the Buddha head ". I relate this image to the artworks of Egypt with the hidden Kundalini science incorporated within.

THE TREE OF LIFE KING PAKAL'S GLYPH

In most of the writings and glyphs that I have seen on the kundalini science, they dealt with what is called " The Tree of Life " ! I have seen this figure shown in many ways. I have explained in other writings how the sofortic superstructure is said to work. When I saw this glyph of King Pakal's sarcophagus lid I instantly knew what it meant. You have to remember that that ancients often wrote spells, or drew glyphs on coffers to direct the dead in their trip through the afterlife. These were roadmaps for the dead. **This could have been very valid if the ancients were waiting for a worldwide Messiah.** On to the depiction.

ANCIENT ALIENS

Some time ago, I saw the television show **ANCIENT ALIENS: EARLY CIVILIZATIONS TO MODERN TIMES** on the HISTORY channel < **HISTORY.COM   1-4229-2148-4 or should I say go to my book store at " spiritualshock.com " >** It was very funny to watch this show. As soon as I saw the artwork I knew what it was. The strange thing about what is being said is what is not being said.

THE BIBLE CONNECTION

We now enter the Bible connection. What is an **ALIEN?** The Bible has fallen or cast down **angels** in it. These cast down **angels** were not from Earth. The Bible has many of them involved in events on Earth. To take this concept a little **further,** there is something called " a wheel upon a wheel " in The Bible in relation to Ezekiel. It is suppose to be some sort of " spaceship ". I quote spaceship because we might not only be talking about distance but also dimensions. **With the introduction of The Bible and biblical concepts to the subject, it takes the alien contact with Earth people called humans to another level.**

FRANK M. CONAWAY, JR.

LUKE 17:21 " THE KINGDOM OF GOD IS WITH YOU "

On one hand you might want to check " satansrapture.com/ezekwheel.htm ". As I have been looking at the kundalini information using The Bible, I would like to say that the meaning of midst is interior.

THE BUDDAH HEAD < NEED TO ADD >

I have ciphered King Pakal's glyph three different times. Maybe I can find one of them for you latter. I call this " the Buddha head " because I do not recall seeing a depiction of the mystical seed < kundalini bird man symbol > opening the skull or that which I called " the hood of Ra " as an Egyptian glyph, but I fell that it is part of the kundalini science.

FIRST KUNDALINI QUESTION

What color was Jesus?

FIRST KUNDALINI QUESTION HINT

What color was Jesus?

Answer: _ _ _ _ T!

AS ABOVE

Look at the internal fish of the human body. To see it clearly you have to cut away the skull and spine. You see the big fish of the upper body above the " little fishes " of the lower self. It is the one of the five hundred thousand. This is true for the kundalinian seed.

LONE RANGER

I just cannot believe this. A new concept to my mind. It is 8-20-2013. Last night I was meditating upon the metaphysical meanings found in the new movie The Lone Ranger < lone equals the one l or " el " >. I was going over a few concepts in my mind. I had found some of the scenes very funny. I began to meditate upon the type of metals that had been shown in the movie. I was reflecting upon the metaphysical said types of metals. I recalled seeing gold, silver, and lead. I was thinking if I had seen any brass. I then began to think about those rabbits. They were very strange. I recalled how big their teeth were. Then I thought about the eating the flesh of the animal, I assume a rabbit, that was being cooked over the open flame. How strange, I had never heard of flesh eating rabbits! I got the joke. It was religious in nature. The rabbit was impaled upon a stake held up by two forks or yods which could symbolize hands. That is enough about that even though there is more that could be said. So I went back to the metaphysical metal types. What about quick silver or mercury? I do not recall seeing any of that. I then thought of iron. The train and rails were made of iron. I was trying to remember another metal when I recalled the Indian head coin used to locate the mountain. I then thought about what was called " a wooden nickel taken from an Indian. I began to laugh when I conceived that the Indian head nickel could be passed off as silver. I was thinking about the rocks of silver which probably had no value to the Indians, I mean who cares? I thought that a Indian might even pay someone to move some rocks out of their way! I then asked myself what was nickel used for? I can't think of anything off hand. A quick look on the internet found at webelements: " nickel is found as a constituent in most meteorites and often serves as one of the criteria for distinguishing a meteorite from other minerals ". I thought back to what the plaque said under the Indian exhibition: " etc ". I then reflected upon what was said about the so called " savages "! I had the Temple of the Great Jaguar in my mind. I thought of the crow on top of Tontoes head as it could be related to the statue on the of the congress building in Washington District of Columbia. King Pakal's sarcophagus lid came to mind. What year is the Temple of the Great Jaguar thought to have been built in? Why? Why what? Hun, what; I'm not thinking what I think I am thinking am I?

PHYSIC TRAMA

In thinking about the whole of this books concepts, I began to ponder upon how a group of people were able to come together to complete a common task. In America it seems that large projects center around some monetary aspect. In conceiving that the Indians had little use for money I concluded that their culture would be the common bond of motiavation. If you think of the ancient free world of the native people, what would there be to buy? Who would you pay rent to? Who does the fish in the stream belong to? Who owns the water? Why not share with your neighbor when you have all there is grown for free? What do you have to plant when nature takes care of that? Why do you have to raise cattle when nature takes care of that? What else could be on your mind but questioning what the source of all of this is? What are the stars and who made them might be the question of the day. What else would or could be the meaning of life? If you think of a huge number of people in one culture with nothing to think about the source of life, you can see how they could gather a lot of mental power towards the subject. What would be their natural nighttime entertainment? They would most likely watch the stars. As they watched the stars night after night, they would remember patterns. These patterns lead us to zodiacal thinking. In noting how the stars were formed at night, added to the awareness of the motion of the Sun and Moon; this would aid a person in traveling about the land and sea. The stars, Sun, and Moon would create a type of celestial map.

CODE OF BEHAVIOR

Current day America is often called " The Great Melting Pot ". That means that the American concept could be a source of great hidden conflict. To put it another way, in America a person is to respect the culture of others no matter how personally offensive it is to them as long as they are not infringed upon. The term infringe is important because to some it means physical contact, while to others it means to accrue in one's accepted environment. That environment could mean street, city, state, or from sea to shining sea. This is important because people interrelate with other people all the time without knowing how the other people " behave "! To put it another way, people just don't know what to expect from other people not of their " specific " culture. I use the term specific because one culture could have several subcultures operating within it. Many ancient cultures had codes of conduct or behavior setup for standards. The term tolerance has to be mentioned because it is this tolerance that really means a deviation from the set norm. This line can become blurred when it comes to orthodox verses unorthodox standards. It is often that this blur which causes the greatest amount of conflict for the person, now has to decide upon by that person if it is to be called right or acceptable. This adds a strange twist about what to expect from a set of circumstances. The same situation could take place several different times all with different outcomes. Take something simple like a date to the movies. As our control set we shall use an example of one person going on ten first dates. At the end of our example set, we could have up to ten different endings to the simple date scenario. While it may not seem like such a big deal, it really is. The experiment demonstrates that the person is dwelling in a highly unstable unpredictable environment. I explain this to show how an environment can distract one's attention.

GET ALONG

As you know, there has been something called slavery involved in the African American experience. It has been suggested several times that it appears that **residual** fallout still accrues in the African American community as a result of physiological damage sustained during the slavery era. It is often suggested that the methods of causing distrust among the slaves towards each other is still at work today. Some have called the techniques use to invoke such distrust among the slaves " The Willie Lynch theory ". I would agree that this concept does still carry some validity, but I feel that it is a very small part of the total picture. This Willie Lynch theory deals with age, color, hair, size, and so on. What is being said is that while the group of former slaves, called " children of the slaves ", have increased in intelligence and social status; they have not been able to overcome silly concepts of induced prejudice. To take it a step further, it is being implied that these " children of the slave " now by free choice can procreate across racial lines, but still find dislike for differences among their own racial group. If this were true, I feel that each African American person would hate every African American person except their own twin. Would you agree with this? If you do, then we must ask as to what else could be the problem?

LOST IN REAL SPACE

Let's deal with the slavery situation from the time of capture < See I was thinking about the African American version. The is slavery in The Bible. I think there were slaves in Egypt. So what was the African mark of Cain stuff about, unless; is Egypt in Africa? Hum! >. For whatever reason, the person has now been captured and enslaved upon their native land. We are not going to deal with who captured them. At this point they are captured. We are not going to deal with the concept of the captors tracking deep into the heart of pitch black Africa and being able to grab a few people while a whole tribe of thousands of people stand by and watch in fear. We are not going to deal with a few sailors taking children from the heart of Africa as thousands of people just watch. We are not going to deal with the concept of a few Europeans just walking into the heart of Africa past lions, tigers, snakes, crocodiles, spiders, quick sand, and who knows what else to just take some African children. Did I forget to mention the cannibals? If that is what they want me to believe, then so be it. What about the grueling temperature? What about the mosquitoes? Then there is the other side of the story. What about the concept that when two tribes would fight; instead of the winners killing the losers, the losers would be sold into slavery. I should have said traded into slavery. As I understand it, the winners were trading the losers for rum. It seems like a pretty good idea. The winners don't have to do a lot of killing. This helps to keep the conscience free. The winners really did the losers a favor by not killing them. The winners get the spoils of war including the take land. The best part of all is that the winners get rum from their new found " trade " partner friends. This sounds like the beginning of a great long term relationship. I wonder what else they may have traded. Maybe the Africans could have gotten their new partners to settle in Africa and carry away some of those stupid rocks. I think the Africans partner / friends still help the Africans to remove the worthless rocks even to today. They came up with a name for the troublesome rocks. They call them diamonds and gold ore.

ENTER THE AMISTAD

My first encounter with a visual concept of the slavery experience was from the movie Roots. The second movie I saw of great significance was called Queen. I believe the most shocking movie of all was the one called Amistad. If I remember right, Amistad was the name of the slave ship. I will pick up the discussion at the point where the " savage " slave is about to board the ship. Now the slave is about to leave their native land never to see it again. The slave is chained to other people that they probably don't know. There is confusion everywhere. The slave catchers are very happy and celebrating because they are being paid for the slaves they are turning over to the ship's captain for transport. Slaves that are still resisting are being yelled at while being beaten. The yelling is in a strange language. Slaves are being inspected for quality and flaws. The slaves are being touched, probed, and violated in all sorts of ways. There is bickering and haggling over price taking place. Some of the settlers families have come to the port for a outing event so to speak. There may be five or more languages being spoken at the same time. Some people involved in overseeing the transaction may be using translators. The boat is being checked for sea worthiness. Supplies are being loaded on the ship. Many of the slaves are crying and yelling. There are rodents moving about. The air has a certain stench in it due to the unclean remnants of deep soaked filth in the wood of the ship! There is a certain smell that some of the sailors emit due to the lack of bathing nor washing their clothes. After all of that is said and done, as the slave is loaded upon the ship, there is a person saying strange words, in a strange language, wearing strange clothes, with some type of majic book, while making hand gestures. They say his title or craft is called priest. The slave is now taken below the deck to be chained in the hull of the ship. The smell is terrible. The air is thick with ammonia laced with germs. The floor is at least ankle deep with fluid. The fluid is comprised of human waste and rotten blood. Slaves whom have never met are locked together. At least for a while the thick air is being treated by the flame and smoke of the torches. It would be nice if they would have at least covered the wood bench with carpet. The journey could have been thought of as a majic carpet ride. Off we go to the new world. The ships slave masters remove the torches and close the hatch. It's pitch black dark in the hull. The acoustics are amplified. The sounds of the wood twisting in the water is greatly amplified. The waves hitting the boat sound like? Due to the size of the boat; the crying, yelling, gasping, and screaming are echoing. There are banging noises coming from above on the deck. These sounds are also greatly amplified. Often the sailors are yelling, who knows what is going on. The slaves can't move so they are going to the bathroom right where they sit. The wood is starting to soften from being saturated. The fluid level on the floor is rising. The density of the ammonia is increasing. Is this a amusement park ride or what?

I think it is " or what " because the journey might last thirty days or more! Good, now the hatch opens; but the sudden flood of light is blinding. It's time to eat. Look, it's the ships special, a mouth full of slop off of a spoon licked by hundreds of people that I don't know. Some of the slaves are brutalized for their attitudes, while others are beaten just because. Look, they are unchaining a few of the lucky slaves. The sailors are taking them up on deck. Maybe they just need some fresh air. No, they will get a firsthand look at the sharks that follow the ship. Those slaves are dead, so over they go! Splash! So much for the cruise vacation ship theory. Back to the darkness of the hull as the hatch closes. Every once in a while a slave is take up upon deck. The movie Amistad showed that in many cases instead of it being one of the " Nubian queens ", it was one of the little boys! Can you believe that! That is the code of behavior that I was talking about. So here we have the slaves emerged in a horrible environment, hermetically sealed in a sensory deprivation device which is called the hull of a ship; but is also referred to as The Belly of the Beast! This next part is going to relate to the origins of the pyramid builders. So the ship lands in the new world. The slaves that did make it are now inspected for wear and tear. As when any live stock is take to market, the product is shined up to give the best appearance for the sale called a auction. The reverse process takes place as when the slave enters the ship. The ship has landed in the new world. The question is which new world? The ship could be anywhere: Europe, North America, South America; anywhere! Here is a question: " which way is up? " I ask this because if the African slave is taken from below the equator and is taken to a place above the equator, the slave might not recognize the star grouping where they end up. This is called to be disorientated. Quite often people try to compare the African American or African European experience to the experience of the native North American. While the two on face value seem to be related, they are totally not anywhere near equal in value. The native North American always knew where they were due to the familiar star pattern. While California is on the other side of America when compared to Virginia, the star constellation pattern can still be perceived. That statement is not the same as comparing the star pattern of Maine to the lower parts of Africa. The slave would have the reface of the Sun and Moon; but what else could help guide them home? I don't have a clue. The sailors were moving across the waters based upon star locations as the made the transit. The captain may have used fifty different calculations to complete the journey. The slave would be trying to figure out how to get from point A to point B when they don't know where point B is. Not only do they not know where point B is, they don't know what fifty points were used in between A and B to guide the ship. The slave is lost in another world! Just then the slave would notice how strange this new world was. There would be several unfamiliar sights in this environment. There would be odd plants and trees. The most shocking things of all would be the unknown animals. There are no lions, but there is a horned fuzzy haired small elephant type. The slave masters call it a buffalo! What is that and how does it behave? Is it a man eater? What type of bugs are these and are they eatable? The slave is just simply lost! So we now have several different cultured Africans coexisting with several types of European people; but what about the very strange third group of people? They are called Indians by the Europeans. Who are those strangely dressed folks. There seems to be a tension between the Indians and the Europeans. To make the situation worst, the Indians seem not to be all of the same culture. It appears that some of the Indians are friendly with the Europeans, while other Indians seem to hate the Europeans. To make the matters worse, there is a subgroup of Europeans that have certain religious ideas that they are trying to impose upon everyone. This religious group secretly teaches the slaves how to read something called hymns from a special book. To some their rituals seem to be some form of majic. This religious subgroup of Europeans are referred to as " missionaries ". The **missionaries** are always talking about saving souls and escaping to a place called Heaven. This Heaven is said to be a place beyond the stars. Some of the slaves have concluded that the Europeans are a combination of star people from Heaven and middle Earth dwellers whom have come to the surface of Earth from their home land called Hell. In a strange twist, the two European groups both have invisible leaders. The leader of the Heaven Europeans title is The Lord. To the Europeans that know The Lord personally, they refer to him as Jesus. The leader of the place called Hell; the Europeans call Satan, Lucifer, or The Devil. It appears that the two subgroups of Europeans are at a type of war called Spiritual! Oh I almost forgot to tell you about another subgroup of the Europeans. There is a religious group of Europeans that are called The Jews. Of the group called The Jews, they are divided into what is called Orthodox and Unorthodox sects. This is very confusing. The Europeans say that the leader of Heaven is part of the group called The Jews. There are said to be many type of Jews based upon different belief systems, look it up yourself. For some reason certain groups of The Jews turned against the leader of Heaven when it was said that he changed from being known by all as The Lord to being known by some as Jesus. It seems that The Jews whom are a subset of the Europeans began to argue if the person whom was called Jesus was the same The Lord. This The Lord was said to be The King of The Jews by some of the European Jews. In reference to the Jesus being The Lord topic, The European Jews were divided into three groups of opinion. One group said that Jesus The Jew was The King of The Jews. Another grouping of The Jews felt that the Jesus person was not The Lord which is said to be the ruler of The Jews. Due to this disagreement The Jews turned the Jesus person over to the Romans to be executed. The Romans at the time were taxing The Jews because the Romans had conquered The Jews. The third division of The Jews were not sure about if the person called Jesus was The Lord or not. By the time of slavery, the Roman world superpower was gone. Christianity, after the order of Jesus is The Lord, had become a dominate European religious and political superpower. The group called The Jews were free people and were involved in various countries economic systems. North America had been the land of the Native Americans who were called Indians. In some ways you could say that until 1492 America was not really included in the European mindset experience. Once the great discovery of 1492 was made, the call for the cultivation of " The Free Land " was made. The flames of greed began to literally burn the American lands. Through many so called shady deals, the Indians were losing most of the North American land to what is called the American Immigrants. The European immigrants were as I have been told less than unrighteous. As a matter of fact, I have read that many of the people that came to America were criminals. I know that this concept may be hard to conceive, but as a child of the slaves I can believe it. Let me put it another way, at the time of slavery, which was the greater savage; was it the Indian or the African? These immigrants were generally Europeans whom had left their homeland in search of a better lifestyle. While I am at that, they may be some of the people whom were put out of their countries for not being civil. Well I might as well bring it to the door. My research questions how far European travelers could penetrate into Africa anyway? I have heard the concept that the African tribes would often fight each other. Instead of killing the captured, the Africans would " trade " their hostages for rum. In the early stages of the relocation, the immigrants were to be setting up colonies for their mother land. Think of it as a goodwill effort made by the wolf in sheep's clothing. The root concept behind the colony idea was to explore the new land in search of exportable natural resources. Included in the exportation system was also a system of " taxing " the colonies for the sake of supporting the motherland. What did this mean to the Indians?

FRANK M. CONAWAY, JR.

THE LONE RANGER CIPHER < NOT ADDED >

Is that really the cipher of The Lone Ranger movie or what.

THE LONE RANGER CIPHER MEANING

< NOT ADDED BUT NOTE: SACKAJUWEA & POKAHOTASS >

NON SENCE

All of a sudden this is starting to make sense. I would like to start off by telling a story. I was riding down a certain street one day and noticed a piece of artwork in the window. I did not have a lot of time on that day, but I did stop to look in the store. I remember saying to myself " un hun ". The lady that work in the store asked if she could help me. I told her that I really didn't have a lot of time, but that I would come back. I don't really want to say this, but I felt like she gave me the " I have heard that a thousand times before " look! I gave her my " and you don't know me nor how I roll " look! With the exchanged of facial nonverbal communication I left the store. I returned about two days later and it seemed as if the lady and I were somehow talking without saying a thing. It was as if she had something to say to me without saying it! I now know what it was. I had not walked into a store so to speak, but rather it was a portal to a new level of knowledge. You could go as far as saying that I had stepped into a star gate.

STAR GATE

We are going to get back to nonsense in a few. This was a very special store. At first I was a little uncomfortable. I felt this way because the place was weird. I need to explain what I mean to you. Suppose you had never been to a chemistry lab and someone took you there blind folded. What do you think that you would think about that situation? The same chemistry lab could be considered good or evil! The good or evil depends upon your mind set. In other words, what is it that you intend to do with the knowledge of chemistry. The same was true of this place. I walked around the store just looking at this and that. It was as the lady was playing the " you're getting closer " game with me in her mind. She had already asked me if I needed any help. I told her that I would just like to look around. I was getting closer. Then there I was. I was looking at a wall of over 125 video lectures. I guess I became engulfed in the titles. I was just absent minded about the whole situation. My mind was kind of blank. I knew that I was looking at something, but I did not know what I was looking at. I guess I can best describe my emotion as " baffled ". How could there be over 125 video titles of various subjects that I had never heard of? Well now that I think of it, I guess that it would not be that hard at all. I guess it was like walking into a part of a library that you had never been in before. Now that I think of it, it was like I had walked into a part of a library that I had never been in before. The section was called " Metaphysics ". If I was talking about superstring structures my " friends " would look at me as if " I " was lost in space. As a matter of fact, that is how most people were looking at me. Some people even had the attitude that because they had never heard of Metaphysics that " I " was some type of special idiot! Looking back, I am getting a real good laugh at that. Why? Because it's very funny! Like I'm some kind of idiot or something. That's why they had a record called " Funk That ".

EUROPEAN KUNDALINI

I think it is important to point out that the science of the kundalini is found in non European cultures. I say this so one can be mindful of concepts generated by the European way of thought. Let me put the situation to you like this, my research states that one of the main cultures that deal with the kundalini subject has been doing so for thousands of years. In their school of thought, the student of kundalini science may have to study for some twenty or so years. Grave warnings are given about the potential dangers of attempting the kundalini exercise. These warnings extend beyond dangers to the physical body, but they also include the possibility of mental and spiritual damage. The ancients whom have written upon the subject have been very clear about such dangers. They even go as far as warning the potential kundalini student about worldly dangers that would cross over into the spiritual realm. In the culture that I am speaking of, the kundalini science is considered to be of the highest order of knowledge that a human can obtain. I find it strange to hear some modern day European self proclaimed experts saying some of the things that they are saying. Knowledge of the kundalini is of the order of you have done it or you have not. Any student of a physical science can tell you that when dealing with scientific experiments, the theory of a process can greatly vary from the practical application. What I am saying is that there may be errors that accrue with any experiment. The same could be said for the kundalini experiment.

THE INNER JOURNEY

According to some of the ancient texts, the kundalini energy path could be opened in two ways. One way is stated to be the best path. This way is called the straight path. The path is said to be made straight < opened > by great and deep < years > spiritual work. The second path that is described is called the **crooked < winding >** path. This is said to be the energy path of the kundalini when sufficient spiritual work has not been done by the student. It should be noted that long before the student attempts to " open " the kundalini energy path, it is traditionally suggested that the student begins to do energy building and control exercises. This energy building has little to do with strength, but it deals with what is called " physic " energy. This is the energy said to be of the chakras. The charka " system " is said to deal with a whole different energy frequency than is used in daily external man's life. There is a whole subset of the kundalini science that deals with the balancing of the individual chakras and the whole chakra system. In the concept of the crooked kundalini path, it is considered that the student of the kundalini has to adjust the kundalini path metal manually as the energy is moving. There are said to be several paths of imbalance that the energy could take. This is where the great danger takes place. The kundalini exercise is dangerous enough by itself. I am not talking about those dangers. If I were reading this, I would ask what type of dangers could I be talking about? In the kundalini opening there is something called the mystic coma. It is called the mystic coma because the student cannot breath. It is like being held under water too long. What happens when you are held under water too long? You breath in water and drown. Let me explain the mystical coma to you another way. What happens when a person runs out of air. Suppose they are locked in a bank vault like in the movie Harlem Nights. Eddie Murphy explains how the men must control their breath in order not to use up the air too quickly. You need to know that this being locked in the bank vault would most likely be a truly terrifying event. There would be a great deal of physiological trauma. Panic could accrue at any time. The men's minds would start to play tricks on them. Visions are subject to be seen as their eyes adjust to the darkness.

Sounds are subject to be heard as the ears become increasingly sensitive to the quiet. The sound of their own heart could be as loud as a banging bass drum. By focusing on the sound of the heart beating, this could also destabilize a calm mindset causing a panic attack. Remember that a panic attack will cause more air to be used inefficiently. These people had not gone through any type of extensive training to deal with such a situation. You are talking about dealing with a sudden altered state of consciousness. You might want to see the 1980 movie Altered States starring William Hurt. This is where the yogi training comes into play. Remember that most times the yogis have trained for many tens of years, and they always do not succeed! If you want to take the subject lightly just look up " alter ego, kundalini, yoga, and altered state of consciousness " on Wikipedia. You can be the judge of how intense the subjects could be! Back to the concept of the mystical coma. I had never read anything about the mystical coma, so I guess the past yogi masters that had went through this just didn't want to ruin the surprise. Sure it was a surprise. You can't breathe in or out! Does that sound funny? Does that sound like something you would volunteer for? This is what I am saying about these new people and their comments, how do they expect to engage the kundalini sequence if they don't use a know kundalini breathing pattern? I shall not go further into the logistics of some of their concepts due to the just ridiculous nature of the concept. Before I go on, I should say that I had read the yogis warn that a student of kundalini could get lost in the meditation. I decided to play a certain album that I felt that I could follow. I figured that the meditation could take the student so deep, that the students mind would lock like a broken record that just kept skipping to the same place over and over again. First I played a track that was of a special tone. This was a kind of notice to my system that I was about to start. May people whom meditate listen to special tones to calm the mind. After I had played the tone, I went on to the album. I looked at the album like a like that you leave when you enter a maze. Once the music was playing, I began to start the breathing pattern. So the student starts the meditation by using a certain breathing pattern. I am not saying that there is only one breathing pattern, I am saying it is the pattern of the students choice or schools teaching. Great we have gotten to the point of the mystical coma. The student now notices that they can't breathe. Yah right! Yes panic hits the student hard and fast because the breathing pattern is suddenly interrupted. Dah, the student can't breathe! I thought the kundalini exercise was all about breathing and so on. You know, the joy of the breath! It is about the joy of the breath, the breath that you don't have! Wait my hearing is different. It is like listening to people talk while you are under water. You notice that your nose has closed. Now might be a good time to call this exercise OFF! Now there is a new problem. You can't open your eyes. It's like one of those dream states where you have almost fallen asleep. You are conscious but you can't move your body. If you have ever had that to happen then you will understand what I am talking about. To make that example even worse, suppose you have the blanket near your nose. You detect a change in air flow which can cause you to panic. Has that ever happened to you? Just think if it happened when you could get no air at all! It seems to be a good reason to PANIC! This is where the yogi mind set training comes into effect. I am calling it a yogi's mind set, but you find that type of mental training in other Asian art forms. Suddenly the student starts to breath. No, the poles have reversed. The different art forms have different names for this type of breathing. I shall use the term reverse breathing or breath. It sounds as if I am suggesting that instead of breathing in or inhaling, the student breaths out or exhales. No, that is not the case. It seems that when the lungs become empty of oxygen, that oxygen flows from the body to the lungs to be channeled to the most vital parts of the human system: the brain! If the student is aware, they would feel the pressure reverse flow. I doubt that the reverse in flow would be noticed if the student was in a state of panic. I think a panic attack at this point would be called to freak out! I think this is why I have always seen it suggested that a trained yogi be with the student when they attempt to open the kundalini coil. Panic could really mean physical or brain death. It is known that a prolonged lack of oxygen to the brain can cause brain death. The person whom that condition befalls is generally called to be in a state of vegetation. This is a very serious art form. So at this point oxygen is reversing its flow into the lungs. The eyes, ears, nose, and mouth lock shut. The lower gate closes which puts pressure upon the prostrate pump. The prostrate pump begins to tremble then **pulse.** This **pulsing creates a vacuum in the testes or lower spheres.** This vacuum causes the sexual fluid to reverse its path. What I mean is the sexual fluid takes its normal path. The symbolic image for the prostrate " **paths** " could be two fork in the road paths placed one on top of the other. If you are thinking what I think you could be thinking, then you might have the right idea. You could make one of the paths form a Y. The Y could be symbolically represented as a triangle. Because the prostrate pump could be said to work in two positions, with each direction of operation in the opposite direction; then the functions of the prostrate pump station could be two triangles woven together pointing in different directions. If you wanted to be clear about the message of the symbol, you could color one triangle white and the other one black. The two paths are the one to reproduction called sexual, and the other path to self reproduction called the spine. The fluid from the spine feeds the brain. As the prostrate pump begins to fire, the side of the jaws also start to tremble. The action starts to draw on they which are called ductless glands. This drawing action causes increased pressure upon the mouth closure. It is as if the mouth was glued closed. It gets worse. The pressure placed upon the teeth cause their nerve endings to become active. When I say to become active, I mean that they tingle. This stimulation cause the student to clamp down even harder upon the teeth. It feels as if the teeth are made of soft plastic. The student should be warned that this can cause many hair line cracks in the teeth. The fluid that accumulates in the mouth is swallowed into the stomach. It seems as if because the stomach is now being given attention that the stomach now becomes active in the drama. The stomach muscles begin the contract. This in a way presses upon the lower lungs. It also does something else, it pulls on the spinal column. This motion helps to move the spinal disks around just enough to find a way for the fluid to **seep thru.** It seem that as the fluid finds a opening thru one disc, that area pressurizes searching for the next opening up the spinal ladder. Because the spine is being pressurized, the oblongate at the neck starts to close. This takes place by the chin lowering onto the chest. There is so much pressure being applied by the chin that the neck locks. The student may hear cracking in the back of the neck area. Then the shoulders budge upward to create that which could be called a turtle neck. There is a definite feeling of fluid moving up the spine. As a matter of fact, there may be a feeling of having to go to the bathroom but you just can't. The mouth is being flooded with fluid. The side jaws are drawing hard on the ductless glands. You can hear the sound of the pressure increasing from the jaws flapping. The jaws make this very weird sound. I know of someone in my family whom use to make that noise all the time. You can feel the special fluid being drawn from the two spheres below. They start to run like rivers in reverse. The student may notice a terrible sound. Imagine you were in a deep dark tunnel and heard this sound. It is the type of sound that would make you squint your eyebrows. You would say to yourself " what IS that! " If you were in a tunnel, good sense would tell you to run. The sound would be like the sound of the water rushing in the Die Hard movie. The sound would also be like that motion shown in the movie The Keep. You could even imagine it sounding like Darth Veda's attack run on the death star in Star Wars. To the student there is nowhere to go! To make it even better, suppose you didn't have a clue what was happening! What is that sound. There is a **buzzing like** hundreds of bumble bees could be heard while electromagnetic sensations move about in one's head. These feelings are coming from the stimulation of the various nerves. All of this is happening. It seems like it's at the same time, although you can also experience each part of the sequence step by step. It is as if as soon as you have time to become aware of one thing, here comes something new. The sound increases in amplitude. It sounds like something is really really really racing towards you in the dark and it is big getting bigger. Using your internal eye, the one that you may know from doing meditation, you focus your attention upon the source of the sound. Isn't this just great, you are looking deeply into internal darkness. Look there is the smallest dot of light that you have ever seen. What is that? It appears to be moving very quickly. It is moving towards your third eye? What, what does that mean? Its moving very erratically. One moment it is at the very end of your optic range, the next it looks like a pebble. Then it looks like a dime size, then moving to the size of a quarter. What is that? The drama I guess has become intense long ago. You can see that it is spinning as it is moving closer to the third eye screen. I should stop here. This is really where the ancient books give a great warning. The ancient texts speak about spiritual work. They call the process to purify oneself. The documents describe terrible internal images that can be seen if the spiritual work is not complete. I don't think that they were talking about becoming a living saint, but I think they meant that the student should have some idea as to what their spiritual perspective is. In other word, some people have a partial spiritual perspective about what they believe. In short, may people don't know what they believe. In the case where the student " sees " one or more of these terrible internal images, the ancients warn that the mind < psychic > could be basically locked by fright. The memory of the image would plague the mind forever. A good movie to see in reference to this Mr. Sardonicus. You almost didn't get this one. I had seen the movie in the early seventies. The movie had an impact upon me. I had thought that Mr. Sardonicus was called Dr. Shalaughagus. Wow, lucky I was able to find it. We shall now go back to our spinning point of light.

IMAGE OF THE CADUCEUS: THE VISION

It looks just like the full white moon, but you can tell that it's spinning. Spinning, yes spinning because there is fire pink and fire blue moving with the rim of the disc as it spins. Hun, it suddenly stops. Guess who's looking you face to face: Kundian < The Happy Ancient Dragon >. **I call her Kundian** < The Happy Ancient Dragon >. **To me she is my " lini ".** What does Kundalini look like? What do you think? The caduceus staff is normally shown with a central pole with two serpents coiled around it. At the to there is often a image of two wings. The two serpents represent the pulsing power of Ida and Pingala. Ida and Pingala sometimes are shown connected to the bottom of the staff. You know that the sign is referring to the kundalini system. How the image is drawn could be used to carry a message or just made to represent the system itself. What I am trying to say is that the caduceus symbol could be made to tell the kundalini story. You have to know that the two dimensional symbol is representing a three dimensional concept. In addition, the image is showing the caduceus system from the side. The caduceus symbol could be thought of as being at a static stop position. Think of a ball that has a name brand written upon it. Now bounce the ball and stop it. Where is the brand label? Keep bouncing and stopping the ball until the brand label is facing the ceiling. How many times are you going to have to repeat this before you get the label facing the ceiling. The caduceus coil is like this. The two serpents appear to be spinning around the pole. In concept, it is the pole that is spinning. This is similar to how a generator makes electromagnetic energy that we call electric. The wings imply that there is vertical, horizontal, and spin rate motions in the caduceus system. It should really be called the caduceus multi coil symbol. Its true place should be inside of a tree of life glyph. You also must consider that the student when doing the kundalini exercise is looking down on the kundalini coil from the inner third eye verses from the front. How, you might ask can the student look down the spine to see the three channels connected to the lowest chakra start to fire? You call it fiber optics. When you look at the frontal image of the caduceus image notice how the serpents expand then contract. If you were looking down upon the caduceus coil as it was firing, where you see the serpents expand you would perceive that the energy pulsed to the point. Think of it like this, let' start with a checker board. You know how the squares are red and black. All we need is one row. Now we expand our row to any number, say one hundred squares. In this example we are going to use a caduceus symbol where as the serpents cross six times. The seventh crossing of the serpents will be where they terminate at the top of the coil. Just for example, we shall call the bottom point of origin square one. Let square, any square, square seven be the second crossing. Let square eighteen be the third crossing. Remember that we are picking these numbers for no reason. This is just an example. What would happen when the lines cross is that the intensity of the electro-magnetic frequency would increase. In other words, the light would appear brighter at the squares where the serpents cross. Not only would the light appear brighter, but it would appear as if the image stopped at that point and then surged forward. It is recorded that images can be seen in the opening of the crooked or straight path. Why do you think that the symbology of serpents is used in the kundalini language? Would your mind be ready for the image of the finial crossing point? The key to the kundalini raising is said to bring the kundalini energy up to the pineal gland. You could think of this in a couple of ways. You could think of the serpent eating the mystical fruit. You could also think of this concept as a serpent eating its own tail. The mystical fruit is the seed of the tree that when energized causes the whole tree to become illuminated. You could think of the mystical fruit as the switch that sends power into the central twelve path acupuncture system. So as the energy ascends up the spine, a vision of a horizontally rotating disc might be seen. At the last stop, or the seventh level the disk would appear to stop. The stop would only seem to be less than a second. Why is this? It would take time for the pineal gland to become saturated / charged with energy. The image that you might see would be of the face of an ancient happy dragon with long whiskers (That is seeing a positive image verses seeing a ugly dragon,

creature, demons, or image. That would not be good while in the state of the mystical coma.

This could be what has been described as causing great psychic damage. This state is said to be able to cause a mental lock. This mind lock is called as being lost inside of one's self.). The colors of flaming pink and blue might surround the image. You might have just enough time to think to yourself " a dragon ", when suddenly the lights go off " dark side of the moon " I guess pitch pit dungeon horror black as the pineal gland becomes fully charged. As your inner eye comprehends that it is suddenly dark, at that moment the lightning wave flashes. This lightning wave flash would be like sitting in space under the full moon. The mind is flooded with " **Black Dot ooze** ", then white light. It is like sitting on a expanding moon disc that turns into a globe of moon light white fire that surrounds the awareness of the self. The crack of a massive lightning strike is heard. The full system is charging. As if this had not been bad enough, there is more.

You might read about tongue placement during meditation. In this case I want to talk about the center of the roof of the mouth. It seem as if something greatly attracts the tongue to that spot on the roof of the mouth. The pressure in the mouth cavity is greatly increased. It is as if the hood or roof of the mouth is trying to collapse. Just then the **tongue** goes wild! The tongue begins to attack the roof of the mouth. When I say attack, I mean that the tongue begins to bore a hole into the flesh of the roof of the mouth. Then the tongue seems to hit bone. The tongue still attacks the bone as the mouth pressure is increased. The tongue flattens out to touch the upper back of the front teeth. Now the flattened tongue makes a type of seal at the tear in the flesh of the roof of the mouth. This seal starts to pressurize the roof of the mouth greatly. Fluid is being drawn from the sides of the mouth, around near the tip of the tongue, over the top of the tongue, into the sealed area, and then swallowed. This action seems to weaken or soften the bone. The reverse pressure becomes extremely great. Then you hear a little something. It sounded like the first crack of the ice of a pond before it shatters. Next you hear one of the strangest sounds you have ever heard. The sound is like a tooth being shattered at the dentist office. Sometimes a tooth will crack into pieces when being extracted. Think of what type of sound an impacted wisdom tooth sounds like if it were to break while the dentist is standing on the chair pulling it out with all he has. CRACK! That is the sound that is heard when that bone breaks in the roof of the mouth. To get an idea of this, you can see the movie **Total Recall** when the implant is removed from the head. Now you swallow bone, flesh, and blood as fluid starts to seep from the hole. It doesn't really **seep,** it is drawn out by the **vacuum** of the mouth. The lower spheres are flowing, as the prostrate is pumping. The fluid is now being drawn up the spine. You seem to feel the fluid moving up the spine like it is being drawn up like in a straw. The fluid being drawn from under the brain by the tongue pump causes the brain to lower. The fluid that flows over the tongue now returns into the hole. This allows the brain to move upward. The process starts again. Soon the spinal cord starts to move. The action is like one of those fishing bobs floating on the water with a cord and hook attached below. The drama continues with a ring of light like that radiating from an explosion. It is not one lightning strike, but the charging of the twelve acupuncture lines at once. As the energy moves from the head down the acupuncture lines, it appears as if a white curtain of pure light is about to fall. When the acupuncture lines are completely charged, the curtain of pure white light does appear to fall. This curtain appears to wrap around the inner body like a mummies bandages. The light dissipates as if the curtain of light were falling. The chin lock at the medulaoblongata starts to release. The ears, nose, and eyes start to release and open. Great the exercise is over, so you think! The sound of thousands of angry bees can be heard. Guess what, they are all coming your way! But what is that? Then you start to feel strange sensations in your head. The sensations move from place to place. What is that all about you wonder? It is the energy charging the different parts of your brain. It is like when the doctor hits your knee with a rubber mallet and your leg kicks out. This is where your yoga posture training and stretching come into play. The next thing you know, your body is starting to contort as the different parts of the brain become stimulated. After you finish contorting, different parts of the brain will be stimulated. If you have something to write with, it is funny to see how your handwriting changes as the different centers of the brain are stimulated. A few hours may pass before you have to go to the rest room. Well you might just notice one of the strangest things of all. The " lower spheres " (FMCJR: Hint) have turned from side to side to front to back! After all of this, now you can spend a great deal of time trying to figure out what that whole exercise was.

WHAT TIME IS IT

I would like to talk a little about time. I am looking at the Baltimore Jewish Times magazine. It has a date on it of October 11, 2013. Under that date, the Hebrew date of 7 Cheshan 5774 is given. I have been told that this large number is the number of years ago was creation.

RETURN TO CARL MUNCK

You might not like this as much as me. Naw, I doubt that seriously. I have to cipher the three disc set again? Oh come on!

ADAMIC RED RACE

"' Adam ' (FMCJR: Adam Kadmon) is both the proper name of the first human and a designation for humankind. God himself gave this appellation to Adam and Eve (Gen. 5:1-2). The color red lies behind the Hebrew root Adam [; 'a]. This may reflect the red soil from which he was made. (From: biblestudytools.com) " As you may all ready know, a lot of my work deals with that which is called in one tradition The Kundalini System. I shall say here what I have commented about several times before. The Kundalini System deals with light frequencies as they relate to the human chakra electro-magnetic energy system. Coming from this frame of reference, I theorize that the " red " relating to Adam relates to his " red root chakra ". Wikipedia says: " Adam is a figure in the Book of Genesis, the Quran and the Book of Iqan. According to the creation myth of Abrahamic religions, he is the first human. In the Genesis creation narratives, he was created by Yahweh-Elohim (' Yahweh-God ', the god of Israel). " I would like to note that the page list Adams spouses as Lilith and Eve. Adams children are listed as: " Cain, Abel, Seth, Awan, Azura, and Rocail ".

ADAMS WIFE: LILITH

It's about to get strange (all up in here)! So when were the teachings about Adams first wife suppose to have been talked about? Awan: " according to the Book of Jubilees, Awan was the wife and sister of Cain and the daughter of Adam and Eve (From Wikipedia)". Enoch is listed as the child of Cain and Awan. " The Book of Jubilees, sometimes called Lesser Genesis (Leptogenesis), is an ancient Jewish religious work of 50 chapters, considered one of the **pseudepigrapha** by Protestant, Roman Catholic, and Eastern Orthodox Churches. Jubilee is considered canonical by the Ethiopian Orthodox Church as well as Bete Israel (Ethiopian Jews), where it is known as the Book of Division. " " The dating of Jubilees has been somewhat problematic for biblical scholars. While the oldest extant copies of Jubilees can be assigned on the basis of the handwriting to about 100 BC, there is much evidence to suggest Jubilees was written prior to this date. For example, the author of Jubilees seems to be aware of 1 Enoch's '

Book of Dreams ', of which , the oldest extant copy (DSS-13 4Q208) has been carbon dated to ca. 200 BC. (From Wikipedia) < T/L > "

MAP TIMELINE: < T/L >

When I was reviewing the information presented by Carl Munck, I began to feel very strongly that I needed to make my own research timeline. I guess I will start here and see how this goes. No, that seems a little confusing. What I will do is note recording the given time by < T/L >, and I will keep a running list at the end of the book. Great, after the book is done I can keep the record on the web as I increase it!

WRITE LETTER

October 28, 2013

ANCIENT ALIENS

Dear Sir,

I am writing about a few issues that were brought up in season 5,volume 1 of the Ancient Aliens television show. The questions I would like to address are: 1) the mystery of the sphere called a monolith on Phobos, which is said to be one of two moons that orbit the planet Mars, 2) the concept of ancient " aliens " whom have visited Earth, and 3) the pyramid / obelisk / sacred site mystery.

Phobos is said to have been discovered on august 18, 1877 by Asaph Hale. Wikipedia says that it was named after the Greek god Phobos which means " fear ".

Some of the known space missions to Mars include: 1) Mariner 9 in 1971, 2) Viking 1 in 1977, 3) Mars Global Surveyor in 1998 & 2003, Mars Express in 2004, 2008, and 2010. " In 2007, the Canadian Space Agency funded a study by Optech and the Mars Institute for an unmanned mission to Phobos known as Phobos Prime (Phobos Reconnaissance and International Mars Exploration). A proposed landing site for the PRIME spacecraft is at the ' Phobos monolith ', a bright object near Stickney which casts a prominent shadow. " Wikipedia states that the Phobos monolith is " a boulder about 85 meters (279 feet) across. "

Does the title War Of The Worlds sound familiar? From windows2universe.org: " July 14, 1965, the first successful flyby of the planet Mare . Returned pictures of Martian surface . Closest approach: 9912 kilometers. Returned 22 images. " The site notes that it is more than just America going to Mars. Anybody could have done anything way out there. There are many choices of how this " monolith might have gotten to the surface of Phobos. Just for the sake of this exercise, let's say the Phobos monolith is really a rock that is not part of Phobos. We are going to agree that someone didn't shave down the surface with a laser or something just to leave this " mark ". By agreeing that this monolith is a rock, we rule out that it could be a type of station with maybe an inflated astrodome type cover to protect the instruments from space dust. We also agree that it is not a huge Styrofoam half sphere used to mark the moon planet and also to be a beacon or guide marker. It could be a type of " X marks the spot " reference point.

THE MARK

I use the term mark because I am thinking about how a country would " claim a planet. I recall that in history, when a country was said to have discovered a new land, the explorers would plant the flag of the nation that they were representing in the discovery. This claim would be exercised even if people were found living on the new found land! The whole moon planet Phobos has been mapped with crater coordinates included.

In an July 22, 2009 interview with C-Span, Buzz Aldrin referred to the Phobos monolith. It is stated on Wikipedia that Phobos rotates once in seven hours thirty nine point two minutes. The article goes on to say: " when people find out about that they're going to say 'Who put that there? Who put that?' The universe put that there. If you choose, God put it there '". The Phobos monolith is described as " a boulder about 85meters (279 feet) across". From dimensionsinfo.com we find " the size of the Space Shuttle Endeavor gives it a maximum payload of 55,250 pounds (25,060 Kilograms). The payload by specifications are 15 foot by 59 foot (4.6 meter by 18 meters)."

ABOUT 279 FEET DIAMETER

We are given the value of 279 feet in diameter for the Phobos sphere. The diameter would be the same even if it is a dome half sphere. It does seem somewhat strange that it appears to be half way sunk into the planet surface? Just for the sake of this discussion, we are going to say that the monolith is about half way penetrated below the surface of Phobos. It does seem like a hard problem? Not really! On ask.com it is stated that " the biggest spacecraft to ever be built is the Atlantis Space Shuttle. It was built in 1997 by the United States government and it made its maiden mission in 1985 which lasted for 293 days in space. It should be noted that the Cassini-Huygens spacecraft (probe) was launched October 15, 1997 upon the Titan IV (401)B rocket. As of 10/30/13, internet research says that the Cassini-Huygens " probe " is the largest payload to be taken into space. At this point we should add, that we are being told about and know of. On nasa.gov, the topic is referred to as the Cassini Solstice Mission. They say " it is one of the largest interplanetary spacecraft ever built, and the third heaviest unmanned spacecraft ever launched into space. The spacecraft is about the same size as a 30-passenger school bus. It weighs roughly 5,650 kilograms (6 tons), more than half of which is rocket fuel. **" I am going to add this in because it may relate to The Great Pyramid at Giza's design. " The Italian Space agency built the high-gain communication antenna. The antenna can transmit in four frequencies at the same time, and was even used as an umbrella! That was done to protect the instruments from the strong sunrays during the early part of the mission – when Cassini was closer to the Sun. That's why the antenna is painted white! "**

CONCRETE ANSWER NUMBER ONE

Since our Ancient Alien show was so kind to include the tests that say that the Earth spheres of " rock " were manmade cast from molted materials, here we have one clue. I think this clue is a " misdirection " technique. Other episodes of this series talk about magic verses illusion. I was sitting there thinking about these stupid spheres forgetting my own work. Dah! An Enigma Solved, how did they carve the pyramid stone? The key misdirection is the word carve. The stones were cast. Note: come on man! Sphere, cube, egg as in alabaster; how about it is a casted material like concrete or new age space foam.

CAST STONES FUNNY PYRAMID

Wow, how did they make those curves? They were part of the mold. How did they get those blocks way up there with no cranes? They walked the raw powered material up the unfinished building and poured that material into the cast like sand on the beach. Sometimes they would make cells to pour first in a very large project like what was done at Hover Dam. What happens if they made the wrong shape? You would just chip it away. You turn the reduction of the rock into a party. We call this a tradition. If the stone, or temple was soft enough, you get two fellows to saw it apart. I know that you think I am joking, but many years ago I was looking at a tape on Aswan (get it? Like the bird) dam I think. The narrator was talking about a temple that had to be moved. The temple was described as been taken apart piece by piece. There were two African Arab type looking fellows using one of those huge long lumber jack saws to cut that temple stone. They were just sawing and smiling. Was the blade cutting the rock? It looked as if the men had takes a red hot knife to a cold stick of butter. I was not sure what I was looking at. I think that I may have been attacked by a form of " spiritual shock ". In the end, they were sitting on the cut temple rock, looking at the camera, looking at me **thru** the television while smiling! Very funny! I Just want to say here: " SILLY RABBIT! " Alright, someone found a giant sphere and took it up to space on a rocket. It's the giant sphere that chased Indiana Jones out of the **Temple Of Doom** at the beginning of the movie. Well while we are at it, the Face On Mars was carved with the space laser umbrella. You saw the space laser umbrella in the movie Diamonds Are Forever. No, you don't like the idea of a mobile space laser. What about the space umbrella in the movie Highlander? I think it was **Highlander 3**. What about a mounted space laser like in the movie **Austin Powers**. So you don't like the conversion of movie science to real life science? If that is the case, I won't ask about the jet pack that was in one of those James Bond movies. I saw it again in a episode of Gilligan's Island. No, too much science fiction? Then I won't mention that Michel Jackson flew off of stage wearing one at the end of one of his concerts. I think it was the Beat It tour. You want to ask about chipping away at a large 100 ton man made rock don't you? How can you move it? You shatter it. You heat the rock for several days. Why not have a festival. Have all the people of the village gather fire wood. Make the fire at the base of the rock. The fire can be small. When I say small, I mean what you would call a barn fire. You should keep the fire going for several days. Of course you can't get into the middle of the fire, or maybe you can if you built a large fire with a path to the rock in the middle. Note, pyramid is said to mean fire inside, or in the middle meaning the inners. You want heat to become trapped in the rock. An idea would be to make the fires large at the outer ends. This will help to trap the heat at the midpoint of the rock between the two fire high points. The heat should travel inward and outward from the two flame high points. It is the inward heat path that we are dealing with now, but place water containers near the outer ends of the flame. We are planning to run or direct the heat within the rock. As the rock spans away from the flame, we might dig a trench at the rocks face. Place water containers near the outer ends of the trench. I like the trench idea. Instead of making a path to run up to the wall, dig a trench to and under the wall. Just as a note, you might want the trench to be twice as far from the wall as the wall is high. No, I know that the wall won't crack when you pour the water into the trenches, but I'm not going to take that chance. I know, you think that it would be your luck for a huge piece to get ejected from the top when / if the wall cracks. I know you think the piece of rock will come flying your way. Maybe you have the **Slep Roc** luck! Days go by and still your tribe keeps the fire going. Sure you've been cooking on the fire. This is called to have a barbeque. Let the ashes simmer down. The brave souls of the village even can get an early for of leg waxing. Let the people run across the hot ash. If the heat burns the hair off of their legs, they can rub the oils and fats on them. Well, it's time for a new party to start. In this party, the people run up to the stone and throw water upon it. The stone gives off steam like an original steam bath. If you think in a tribal nature, you could start to divide the people up into teams. From there you could easily subdivide the teams to attend certain tasks like gather kindling, collect water, and dig the trenches.

ROCK MY WORLD

Well the idea of putting rocks at the base of the rock wall came to mind. We would do this to help concentrate and contain the heat under the fire. The built up rocks would also create air pockets which would become super hot. We gather rocks for the base of our fire. Just add water and see what happens! Magic? No, science! Now back to the rock on Phobos. What we are looking for is an rock object that has a radius of 85 meters or more. Have any ideas where we might find one just laying around? " Methone is a very small natural satellite of Saturn lying between the orbits of Mimas and Enceladus. " " In May 2012, the Cassini spacecraft obtained its first close-up photographs of Methone, revealing an egg-shaped moonlet with a remarkably smooth surface, with no visible craters. The moons Pallene and Aegaeon are thought to be similarly smooth. " " Methone's mean radius is 1.6 kilometer. " One kilometer is equal to 3,280.8399 feet. " Methone was discovered by the CICLOPS Team on June 1, 2004. " Methone is almost twelve times as large as the monolith on Phobos (3,280.8399 divided by 279 equals 11.759282795698). Too big even if we cut it in half (that's a joke, like solstice could be ciphered as: sol – s – t – ice. Sol for star [called the Sun] system – s for the curves in the motion of the planets about the Sun star which make elipes – t meaning one sector of more than one sectors called systems – and ice meaning when you get away from Sol it is cold out there in deep space until you get near another star)! We need another rock. Maybe we could take the raw rock material up into space in a shuttle. We could design an inflatable bag type half sphere of which we could inject with the raw materials in a mix that will harden in space. We leave the object in space to cool and hope no one steals it while we are gone. We come back sometime later and attach a rocket to our space bag. The rocket tows the space bag out to Phobos. The rockets place the object at just the right point called a window. The space bag falls to Phobos. No, we better make it a sphere. There is no belly up on a sphere! The space sphere bag falls to Phobos. Parachutes slow the decent until the bag and chutes catch on fire as planned. The sphere picks up enough speed so that the impact embeds the sphere deep into the measured dense surface and dust. That means that we know how thick the dust is and how hard the soil is. You see, we are reducing this to a math problem. Besides, this monolith would kind of say who is claiming the planet. It could be like space chess or something. If you plant a weed called a flag on my planet; "I will just knock it over, with my space rover"!

ROCK ON

That is a lot of material to be hauling out into space. It seems that this would be the true meaning of having your money go up in flames. What else could we do? When a space rock hits the Earth it's called a meteorite. That seems like that is just what we need. We need an unclaimed meteorite. You just can't go around stealing other peoples space rocks, or can you? I'm sure somebody knows the rules, or at least is in charge of making them up as situations arise. I saw the meteor first! Yes; while that is true, I touched it with my rover robot first! Dang!

MINOR PLANETS

" Asteroids are minor planets, especially those of the inner Solar System. The larger ones have also been called planetoids. " " As of September 2013, the Minor Planet Center had data on more than one million objects, of which 625,106 had enough information to be given numbered designations. " " The U.S. military also declassified the information that its military satellites, built to detect nuclear explosions, had detected hundreds of upper-atmosphere impacts by objects ranging from one to 10 meters across. " " Among all the automated systems, 4711 near-Earth asteroids have been discovered including over 600 more than 1 kilometer (0.6 miles) in diameter. " " Traditionally, small bodies orbiting the Sun were classified as asteroids, comets or meteoroids, with anything smaller than ten meters across being called a meteoroid. The term ' asteroid ' is ill-defined. It never had a formal definition, with the broader term minor planet being preferred by the International Astronomical Union from 1853 on. (From: Wikipedia) "

NEAR EARTH

" Newly discovered asteroid 2013 TV 135 made a close approach to Earth on Sept. 16. Estimated to be about 1,300 feet (400 meters) in size, the asteroid has a 1-in 63,000 chance of impacting the Earth in the year 2032. " " More than 10,000 asteroids and comets that can pass near Earth have now been discovered. The 10,000th near-Earth object, asteroid 2013 MZ5, was first detected on the night of June 16, 2013, by the Pan-Starrs-1 telescope. (By nasa.gov) "

"' As NASA works through proposals for an asteroid retrieval mission, a new paper shows that there are other research groups considering which asteroids to pick first. One scientific team has identified 12 " Easily Retrievable Objects " in our solar system that are circling the sun and would not cost too much to retrieve (in relative term, of course!). The definition of an ERO is an object that can be captured and brought back to a stable gravitational point near Earth (called a Lagrange point, or more specifically the L1/L2 points between the sun and the Earth.) The change in speed necessary in these objects to make them easily retrievable is " arbitrarily " set at 500 meters per second (1,641 feet/second) or less, the researchers stated.' ' Also, steering these objects around has another benefit: teaching humans how to deflect potentially hazardous asteroids from smacking into the Earth and causing damage. As we were reminded about earlier this year, even smaller rocks such as the one that broke up over a portion of Russia can be hazardous.' ' That said, NASA is taking a serious look at the matter, as well as two groups that would like to mine asteroids: Planetary Resources and Deep Space Industries. For the curious, this is the complete list of possible asteroids: 2006 RH120, 2010 VQ98, 2007 UN12, 2010 UE51, 2008 EA9, 2011 UD21, 2009 BD, 2008 UA 202, 2011 BL45, 2011 MD, 2000 SG344, AND 1991 VG.' (From: technology.org) " " A new private company called Deep Space Industries announced today that it intends to send a fleet of small spacecraft to near-Earth asteroids with the aim of mining resources and turning them into products using space-based 3-D printers. (From: wired.com by Adam Mann 03.29.13) " I wonder how many of those " small spacecraft can fit in a space shuttles bay? I just felt that I wanted to add this: " The average speed of an asteroid is 25 kilometers per second, which is almost 56,000 miles an hour. Asteroids can gain much greater speed than that, however. For example, the closest known asteroid to the sun, JG6, Designated an asteroid 2004, travels at a speed of around 67,000 miles per hour. (From: answerbag.com) " Meteoroids are significantly smaller than asteroids, and range I size from small grains to 1 meter wide objects.

TIMELINE

THE ADAMIC RACE

" What is the approximate date that the Genesis / Adam and Eve story took place? "

'4004 BC: " 9:00 AM Oct. 23,4004 BC as calculated by 17C Irish British James Ussher (Yr.) and refined by James Lightfoot (From answers.yahoo.com) " What is the approximate date that the Genesis / Adam and Eve story took place? " It is of interest to note what another person named " Bluebird " posted: " At least 42,000 years ago God began getting the earth ready for mankind. Genesis 1:1 makes the statement that God created the heavens and the earth. This is not part of the 1st day. It is a statement and we do not know when God did this. After each creative period, the verses say then there was morning and night the first day or even 2nd day etc. But for the seventh day it just says God rested. It does not say it came to an end. We are still in the seventh day. According to the bible, Adam and Eve were created at the end of the sixth day in 4027 BC. If you add our current year plus one because there is no zero year, you get 6035 years. That is how long the seventh day has lasted so far. So it would seem logical that the previous days were as long if not longer. At the end of this day of rest, God will restore the earth to the paradise he intended for it to be in the first place. "

Here is another interesting answer from Jen: " AGE OF EARTH FROM " HUBPAGES @ newwoman54.hubpages " that you can look up if you like. " Around what year were Adam and Eve created? " from BIBLE HUB by BIBLOS.

THE EGO MARK AGAIN

I will just give you another clue as to whom or who has the mark: " REVELATION 13:17 ". The Bible that I am looking at right now at Revelation 13:16 refers to " all the people ".

HOW TO GET WISDOM - JAMES 1:5 REFERED FROM 666 PROPHECY

All I can say at this point is to look up what has been said.

Cross References

1 Kings 3:9
So give your servant a discerning heart to govern your people and to distinguish between right and wrong. For who is able to govern this great people of yours?"
Psalm 51:6
Yet you desired faithfulness even in the womb; you taught me wisdom in that secret place.
Proverbs 2:6
For the LORD gives wisdom; from his mouth come knowledge and understanding.
Proverbs 3:6
in all your ways submit to him, and he will make your paths straight.

Proverbs 8:17
I love those who love me, and those who seek me find me.
Daniel 2:21
He changes times and seasons; he deposes kings and raises up others. He gives wisdom to the wise and knowledge to the discerning.
Matthew 7:7
"Ask and it will be given to you; seek and you will find; knock and the door will be opened to you.

From: Treasury of Scripture Knowledge

If any of you lack wisdom, let him ask of God, that gives to all men liberally, and upbraides not; and it shall be given him.

666 REASON

Based upon on what I have recorded, I would like to " reason " with you about the 666 issue. We find that no one could buy or sell without the mark or name of the beast in their hand or forehead. As far as the hand is concerned, the hand or its deeds rather reflect what the person thinks by telling the hand what to do! From this we can conclude that the hand is the doing part of the expression of the mind which is in the head. We can say that the hand and mind operate as one unit or one in the same. The mark of the beast is stated as being in the hand or the head in our example. The mark of the beast is implied to be of the same order as the name of the beast. Each of these will show themselves by acting from the head thru the hand. If we think of our unit as a whole, we can conclude that the mark of the beast is equal to the name of the beast. We have found a value word equivalent for the numerical value of 666. The value that we have found is a compound word: He-phren. This " He-phren " term should be thought of as saying more than one thing. I am saying that the " He " has a meaning in this compound term, and the " phren " also has a meaning in this statement. By there being two words in the compound word, it should imply that one of the words helps define or modifies the other word.

FRANK M. CONAWAY, JR.

THE SAME OLD CORD

The Bible states that THE LORD is THE LIGHT. The original Adam, who is Adam Kadmon in the Jewish tradition, was created him, her, them. It is this Adam Kadmon who is created in the image of THE LORD GOD.

CHERUBIM OR CHERUBIMS GENESIS 3:24

Genesis 3:24

Viewing the King James Version. Click to switch to 1611 King James Version of Genesis 3:24.

So he drove out the man; and he placed at the east of the garden of Eden Cherubim's, and a flaming sword which turned every way, to keep the way of the tree of life.

- King James Bible "Authorized Version", Cambridge Edition

CAIN THEN

I should note that at Genesis 4:1 Cain is born before Able.

Other Translations of Genesis 3:24

So he droue out the man: and he placed at the East of the garden of Eden, Cherubims, and a flaming sword, which turned euery way, to keepe the way of the tree of life.
- King James Version (1611) - View 1611 Bible Scan

So He drove the man out; and at the east of the garden of Eden He stationed the cherubim and the flaming sword which turned every direction to guard the way to the tree of life.
- New American Standard Version (1995)

So he drove out the man; and he placed at the east of the garden of Eden the Cherubim, and the flame of a sword which turned every way, to keep the way of

the tree of life.
- American Standard Version (1901)

So he sent the man out; and at the east of the garden of Eden he put winged ones and a flaming sword turning every way to keep the way to the tree of life.
- Basic English Bible

And he drove out Man; and he set the Cherubim, and the flame of the flashing sword, toward the east of the garden of Eden, to guard the way to the tree of life.
- Darby Bible

So he drove out the man: and he placed at the east of the garden of Eden Cherubim, and a flaming sword which turned every way, to keep the way of the tree of life.
- Webster's Bible

So he drove out the man; and he placed Cherubs at the east of the garden of Eden, and the flame of a sword which turned every way, to guard the way to the tree of life.
- World English Bible

yea, he casteth out the man, and causeth to dwell at the east of the garden of Eden the cherubs and the flame of the sword which is turning itself round to guard the way of the tree of life.
- Youngs Literal Bible

So He drove out the man; and He placed at the east of the garden of Eden the cherubim, and the flaming sword which turned every way, to keep the way to the tree of life.
- Jewish Publication Society Bible

Wesley's Notes for Genesis 3:24

3:24 God drove him out - This signified the exclusion of him and his guilty race from that communion with God which was the bliss and glory of paradise. But whether did he send him when he turned him out of Eden? He might justly have chased him out of the world, #Job 18:18|, but he only chased him out of the garden: he might justly have cast him down to hell, as the angels that sinned were, when they were shut out from the heavenly paradise, #2Pe 2:4|, but man was only sent to till the ground out of which he was taken. He was only sent to a place of toil, not to a place of torment. He was sent to the ground, not to the grave; to the work - house, not to the dungeon, not to the prison - house; to hold the plough, not to drag the chain: his tilling the ground would be recompensed by his eating its fruits; and his converse with the earth, whence he was taken, was improvable to good purposes, to keep him humble, and to mind him of his latter end. Observe then, That though our first parents were excluded from the privileges of their state of innocency, yet they were not abandoned to despair; God's thoughts of love designing them for a second state of probation upon new terms. And he placed at the east of the garden of Eden, a detachment of cherubim, armed with a dreadful and irresistible power, represented by flaming swords which turned every way, on that side the garden which lay next to the place whither Adam was sent, to keep the way that led to the tree of life.

Comments for Genesis 3:24

K S REDDY's comment on 2013-04-25 00:13:00:

From Wesley notes: "This signified the exclusion of him and his guilty race from that communion with God which was the bliss and glory of paradise."- Is Eden a paradise. I don't find the word in BIBLE up to Genesis 3.

Anthony's comment on 2013-03-27 16:20:17:

Read in the context of Genesis 3:22, The Cherubims represent knowledge of which Adam and Eve had none. They were like innocent children knowing only the bliss in which they lived. In verse 22 God says: And the LORD God said, "The man has now become like one of us, knowing good and evil. He must not be allowed to reach out his hand and take also from the tree of life and eat, and live forever." Both of these refer to their ability to know the difference between good and evil. They could now make a choice. The key question of this significant part of the bible on which the major languages have based their teaching and guidance on in this: Who else was God referring to when he says "now they will be like one of US"?

Wilst's comment on 2012-08-04 00:11:03:

Man is created in the image of God. He is being chased out of the ease of life and out of the fellowship with the Lord for he has sinned. A barrier or limit is created that man must overcome to come back to the presence of the Lord. In this way we see that the folly of God is wiser than the wisdom of man (1 Corinthians 1:25)... and that God has good plans for man (Jeremiah 29:11)

CHERUBIMS

My research shows that the term cherubims occurs 64 times in 57 verses in The King James Bible.

HEBREWS 9:5

WHY DOES THE TERM CHERUBIMS STOP AT HEBREWS 9:5? And over it the cherubims of glory shadowing the mercyseat; of which we cannot now speak particularly.

END OF BOOK

I want to thank you now because this is about the point where you may or may not understand why I am recording what I record the way that I do. All I can say is that at this point the subject at hand is rather intense.

Thank You!   FRANK AKA META 3.14

THE HOLY GHOST AT HEBREWS 9:5

" The Holy Ghost this signifying, that the way into the holiest of all was not yet made manifest, while as the first tabernacle was yet standing: ".

HEBREWS 9:9

Which was a figure for the time then present, in which were offered both gifts and sacrifices, that could not make him that did the service perfect, as pertaining to the **conscience;**

HEBREWS 9:14

How much more shall the blood of Christ, who through the eternal Spirit offered himself without spot to God, purge your **conscience** from dead works to serve the living God?

The Authorized Version or King James Version (KJV), 1611, 1769. Outside of the United Kingdom, the KJV is in the public domain. Within the United Kingdom, the rights to the KJV are vested in the Crown.

LEXICON:G5502

Lexicon :: Strong's G5502 - Cheroub

Dictionary Aids

FRANK M. CONAWAY, JR.

Vine's Expository Dictionary: View Entry

TDNT Reference: 9:438,1312

Outline of Biblical Usage

1. cherubim, two golden figures of living creatures with two wings; they were fastened to the lid of the ark of the covenant in the holy of holies (both at the sacred tabernacle and of Solomon's temple) in such a manner that their faces were turned towards each other and down towards the lid, which they overshadowed with their expanded wings. Between these figures God was regarded as having fixed his dwelling place.

KJV Translation Count — Total: 1x

The KJV translates Strongs G5502 in the following manner: cherubim (1x).

Strong's Number G5502 matches the Greek Χερούβ (Cheroub), which occurs 1 times in 1 verses in the Greek concordance of the KJV.

Hbr 9:5- And over it the cherubims [G5502] of glory shadowing the mercyseat; of which we cannot now speak particularly.

Cherub: From Wikipedia, the free encyclopedia: It has been suggested that Living creatures (Bible) be merged into this article. (Discuss) Proposed since December 2013.

This article is about a type of supernatural being in the Bible. For winged babies in artwork, see putto. For other uses, see cherub (disambiguation)

< Image removed >

St. Michael the Archangel guarding the entrance of the Garden of Eden by Giusto de' Menabuoi ca. 1377.

A cherub, also pl. cherubim, (Hebrew removed, English trans kəruv, pl. kəruvim, dual kəruvayim Latin cherub[us], pl. cherubi[m], Syriac (removed) is a winged angelic being who are considered to attend on the Abrahamic God in biblical tradition. The concept is represented in ancient Middle Eastern art as a lion or bull with eagles' wings and a human face, and regarded in traditional Christian angelology as an angel of the second highest order of the ninefold celestial hierarchy.[1] Cherubim are mentioned throughout the Hebrew Bible and once in the New Testament in reference to the mercy seat of the Ark of the Covenant (Hebrews 9:5).

Origins

The Hebrew term cherubim is cognate with the Assyrian term karabu, Akkadian term kuribu, and Babylonian term karabu; the Assyrian term means 'great, mighty', but the Akkadian and Babylonian cognates mean 'propitious, blessed'.[2][3] In some regions the Assyro-Babylonian term came to refer in particular to spirits which served the gods, in particular to the shedu (human-headed winged bulls);[3] the Assyrians sometimes referred to these as kirubu, a term grammatically related to karabu.[2] They were originally a version of the shedu, protective deities sometimes found as pairs of colossal statues either side of objects to be protected, such as doorways.[3][4] However, although the shedu were popular in Mesopotamia, archaeological remains from the Levant suggest that they were quite rare in the immediate vicinity of the Israelites.[4] The related Lammasu (human-headed winged lions — to which the sphinx is similar in appearance), on the other hand, were the most popular winged-creature in Phoenician art, and so scholars suspect that Cherubim were originally a form of Lammasu.[4] In particular, in a scene reminiscent of Ezekiel's dream, the Megiddo Ivories — ivory carvings found at Megiddo (which became a major Israelite city) — depict an unknown king being carried on his throne by hybrid winged-creatures.[5]

< Image removed >

A pair of shedu, protecting a doorway (the body of the creatures extending into the distance).

The Lammasu was originally depicted as having a king's head, a bull's body, and an eagle's wings, but because of the artistic beauty of the wings, these rapidly became the most prominent part in imagery;[2] wings later came to be bestowed on men, thus forming the stereotypical image of an angel.[5] The griffin — a similar creature but with an eagle's head rather than that of a king — has also been proposed as an origin, arising in Israelite culture as a result of Hittite usage of griffins (rather than being depicted as aggressive beasts, Hittite depictions show them seated calmly, as if guarding),[5] and some have proposed that griffin may be cognate to cherubim,[6] but Lammasu were significantly more important in Levantine culture, and thus more likely to be the origin.[2]

Early Semitic tradition conceived the cherubim as guardians, being devoid of human feelings, and holding a duty both to represent the gods and to guard sanctuaries from intruders, in a comparable way to an account found on Tablet 9 of the inscriptions found at Nimrud.[2] In this view, cherubim, like the shedu, were probably originally depictions of storm deities, especially the storm winds.[6] This view is offered as a hypothesis to explain the reason for cherubim being described as acting as the chariot of the LORD in Ezekiel's visions, the Books of Samuel,[7] the parallel passages in the later Book of Chronicles,[8] and passages in the early Psalms:[2] "and he rode upon a cherub and did fly: and he was seen upon the wings of the wind".[9][10]

In the Bible

Cherubim first appear in the Bible in the Garden of Eden, to guard the way to the Tree of life.[11]

In Isaiah 37:16, Hezekiah prays, addressing Yahweh as "enthroned above the Cherubim" (referring to the mercy seat).

Cherubim feature at some length in the Book of Ezekiel. When they first appear in chapter one, when Ezekiel was "by the river Chebar", they are not called cherubim until chapter 10, but he saw "the likeness of four living creatures". (Ezekiel 1:5) Each of them had four faces and four wings, with straight feet with a sole like the sole of a calf's foot, and "hands of a man" under their wings. Each had four faces: The face of a man, the face of a lion on the right side, the face of an ox on the left side, and the face of an eagle. (Ezekiel 1:6-10)

In Ezekiel chapter ten, another full description of the Cherubim appears with slight differences in details. Three of the four faces are the same; man, lion and eagle; but where chapter one had the face of an ox, Ezekiel 10:14 says "face of a cherub". Ezekiel equates the Cherubim of chapter ten with the living creature of chapter one by saying: "This is the living creature (Hebrew removed) that I saw by the river of Chebar", in Ezekiel 10:15, and in Ezekiel 10:20 he said: "This is the living creature that I saw under the God of Israel by the river of Chebar; and I knew that they were the cherubim."

In a psalm of David that appears in 2 Samuel 22:11 and Psalms 18:10, David said that the LORD "rode upon a cherub, and did fly: and he was seen upon the wings of the wind,".

The words Cherub and Cherubim appear many other times in the holy scriptures, referring to the Cherubim of beaten gold on the mercy seat of the Ark of the Covenant, and images on the curtains of the tabernacle, and in Solomon's temple, including two Cherubim made of olive wood overlaid with gold that were ten cubits high.[12]

Worth noting is also the fact that within the Hebrew Bible the cherubim do not have the status of angels. It is only in later sources (like De Coelesti Hierarchia - see below) that they are considered to be a division of the divine messengers.[13]

Post-biblical Judaism

< Image removed >A cherub, according to traditional Christian iconography.

Many forms of Judaism teach belief in the existence of angels, including Cherubim within the Jewish angelic hierarchy. The existences of angels is generally widely contested within traditional rabbinic Judaism; there is, however, a wide range of views on what angels actually are, and how literally one should interpret biblical passages associated with them.

In Kabbalah there has long been a strong belief in Cherubim, with the Cherubim, and other angels, regarded as having mystical roles. The Zohar, a highly significant collection of books in Jewish mysticism, states that the Cherubim were led by one of their number, named Kerubiel.[2]

On the other end of the philosophical spectrum is the view of Rabbi Moshe ben Maimon, better known as Maimonides. He had a neo-Aristotelian interpretation of the Bible. Maimonides writes that to the wise man, one sees that what the Bible and Talmud refer to as "angels" are actually allusions to the various laws of nature; they are the principles by which the physical universe operates. "Guide for the Perplexed" II:4 and II:6.

> For all forces are angels! How blind, how perniciously blind are the naive?! If you told someone who purports to be a sage of Israel that the Deity sends an angel who enters a woman's womb and there forms an embryo, he would think this a miracle and accept it as a mark of the majesty and power of the Deity, despite the fact that he believes an angel to be a body of fire one third the size of the entire world. All this, he thinks, is possible for God. But if you tell him that God **placed in the sperm the power** of forming and

demarcating these organs, and that this is the angel, or that all forms are produced by the Active Intellect; that here is the angel, the "vice-regent of the world" constantly mentioned by the sages, then he will recoil.

For he {the naive person} does not understand that the true majesty and power are in the bringing into being of forces which are active in a thing although they cannot be perceived by the senses....**Thus the Sages reveal to the aware that the imaginative faculty is also called an angel; and the mind is called a cherub. How beautiful this will appear to the sophisticated mind, and how disturbing to the primitive.**"

Maimonides says (Guide for the Perplexed III:45) that the figures of the cherubaim were placed in the sanctuary only to preserve among the people the belief in angels, there being two in order that the people might not be led to believe that they were the image of God.

Reform Judaism and Reconstructionist Judaism generally either drop references to angels or interpret them metaphorically.[citation needed]

Cherubs are discussed within the midrash literature. The two cherubaim placed by God at the entrance of paradise (Gen. iii. 24) were angels created on the third day, and therefore they had no definite shape; appearing either as men or women, or as spirits or angelic beings (Genesis Rabbah xxi., end). The cherubim were the first objects created in the universe (Tanna debe Eliyahu R., i. beginning). The following sentence of the Midrash is characteristic: "When a man sleeps, the body tells to the **neshamah (soul)** what it has done during the day; the neshamah then reports it to the **nefesh (spirit)**, the nefesh to the angel, the angel to the cherub, and the cherub to the seraph, who then brings it before God (Leviticus Rabbah xxii.; Eccl. Rabbah x. 20).

A midrash states that when Pharaoh pursued Israel at the Red Sea, God took a cherub from the wheels of His throne and flew to the spot, for God inspects the heavenly worlds while sitting on a cherub. The cherub, however, is "something not material", and is carried by God, not vice versa (Midr. Teh. xviii. 15; Canticles Rabbah i. 9).

In the passages of the Talmud that describe the heavens and their inhabitants, the seraphim, of annim, and ḥayyot are mentioned, but not the cherubim (Ḥag. 12b); and the ancient liturgy also mentions only these three classes.

< Image removed >

One traditional depiction of the cherubim and chariot vision, based on the description by Ezekiel.

In the Talmud, Yose ha-Gelili holds,[14] when the Birkat HaMazon (Grace after Meals) is recited by at least ten thousand seated at one meal, a special blessing, "Blessed is Ha-Shem our God, the God of Israel, who dwells between the Cherubim", is added to the regular liturgy.

Middle ages Christianity

In Medieval theology, following the writings of Pseudo-Dionysius, the cherubim are the second highest rank in the angelic hierarchy, following the Seraphim.[15] In western art, Putti are sometimes mistaken for Cherubim, although they look in no way alike.

Depictions

There were no cherubim in Herodian reconstruction of the Temple, but according to some authorities, its walls were painted with figures of cherubim.[16] **In Christian art they are often represented with the faces of a lion, ox, eagle, and man < OR IS THAT A MAN, OR LIKNESS OF A MAN > peering out from the center of an array of four wings** (Ezekiel 1:5-11, 10:12, 21 Revelation 4:8); (seraphim have six); the most frequently encountered descriptor applied to cherubim in Christianity is many-eyed, and in depictions the wings are often shown covered with a multitude of eyes (showing them to be all seeing beings). Since the Renaissance, in Western Christianity cherubim have become confused with putti—innocent souls, looking like winged children, that sing praises to God daily—that can be seen in innumerable church frescoes and in the work of painters such as Raphael.

References:

Jump up ^ **"Oxford Dictionaries: cherub". Oxford University Press. 2013.**

1. ^ Jump up to: a b c d e f g "Jewish Encyclopedia: cherub". JewishEncyclopedia.com, 2002-2011. Original, 1906.
2. ^ Jump up to: a b c De Vaux, Roland (tr. John McHugh), Ancient Israel: Its Life and Institutions (NY, McGraw-Hill, 1961)
3. ^ Jump up to: a b c Peake's commentary on the Bible
4. ^ Jump up to: a b c Wright, G. Ernest, Biblical Archaeology (Philadelphia, Westminster Press, 1957)
5. ^ Jump up to: a b William H. Propp, Exodus 19-40, volume 2A of The Anchor Bible, New York: Doubleday, 2006, ISBN 0-385-24693-5, Notes to Exodus 15:18, page 386, referencing:Julius Wellhausen, Prolegomena to the History of Israel, Edinburgh: Black, 1885, page 304. Also see: Robert S. P. Beekes,Etymological Dictionary of Greek, volume 1, Leiden and Boston: Brill, 2010 ISBN 978-90-04-17420-7, page 289, entry for γρυπος,"From the archaeological perspective, origin in Asia Minor (and the Near East: Elam) is very probable."
6. **Jump up ^** 1 Samuel 4:4, 2 Samuel 6:2, 2 Samuel 22:11
7. **Jump up ^** 1 Chronicles 13:6

8. **Jump up** ^ 2 Samuel 22:11
9. **Jump up** ^ Psalms 18:10
10. **Jump up** ^ Genesis 3:24 (King James Version) at Bible Gateway.com
11. **Jump up** ^ "1 kings 6:23-6:35 KJV - And within the oracle he made two". Bible Gateway. Retrieved 2012-12-30.
12. **Jump up** ^ Kosior, Wojciech. "The Angel in the Hebrew Bible from the Statistic and Hermeneutic Perspectives. Some Remarks on the Interpolation Theory". The Polish Journal of Biblical Research, Vol. 12, No. 1 (23), pp. 56-57. Retrieved 1 December 2013.
13. **Jump up** ^ Berakhot 49b
14. **Jump up** ^ Dionysius the Areopagite's Celestial Hierarchy - See Chapter VII
15. **Jump up** ^ Yoma 54a

Further reading: Yaniv, Bracha, The Cherubim on Torah Ark Valances, Jewish Art Department, Bar-Ilan University, published in Assaph: Studies in Art History, Vol.4, 1999

External links Jewish Encyclopedia: Cherub

Catholic Encyclopedia: Cherubim

The Cherubim - some pointers and problems by Rabbi Dr Raymond Apple

LILITH RESEARCH

Lilith < also liyliyth from the Hebrew number 3915 >

Dictionary Aids

TWOT Reference: 1112
Outline of Biblical Usage

1. "Lilith", name of a female goddess known as a night demon who haunts the desolate places of Edom
    1. might be a nocturnal animal that inhabits desolate places

KJV Translation Count — Total: 1x

The KJV translates Strongs H3917 in the following manner: screech owl (1x).

Gesenius' Hebrew-Chaldee Lexicon Strong's Number [H3917] matches the Hebrew (liyliyth), which occurs 1 times in 1 verses in the Hebrew concordance of the KJV.

Isa 34:14- The wild beasts of the desert shall also meet with the wild beasts of the island, and the satyr shall cry to his fellow; the screech owl [H3917] also shall rest there, and find for herself a place of rest.

LILITH - WHAT IS A SCREECH OWL

It is kind of strange, but the more you know about a subject, the way possible answers come to you. What do you know about Lilith? She is said to be related to Adam before the time of Eve. So Lilith is related to Adam Kadmon in some way. You know that Lilith is not the mother of " living beings "! Some traditions say that Lilith is the killer of babies as in sudden crib death. Without going further into this and that, I will explain what Lilith is. Lilith is a form of kundalini. You can figure out the symbolic meaning of her. The concept is that Lilith is a bird of nest. Lilith guards the place of the male eggs. You could take this a step further. Lilith is the guardian of the way or path to the kundalini path or tree with the fruit of everlasting life. You could even say that the **phallus** and the spinal column are two trees with the same root. Both trees draw from the mystical waters of life. Hence the sign of the **flail**, bent staff, the " v " peace sign, and more. You could even say that Lilith is a powerful female element. No, see this is going to an advanced conceptual level.

THE FORM YOU SEE

I said that Lilith is a powerful " female element ". That may not be true. What I am trying to explain here is that Lilith as Kundalini also show themselves in the way they do so as to fit into the intelligence of the system. This is like when an actor plays a part, the character is just the way the actor is appearing at that time. I hope to write more about this concept as it relates to **Jewish Mysticism**.

LILITH / KUNDALINI

Don't forget that Lilith / Kundalini is the woman of your nocturnal emission. In that case she would be called your first love. It was Lilith that let you know that your sexual energy feeding complex was matured or charged. Back to Lilith / Kundalini being " shown as " an owl. Well, she is a wise old owl! How do you know if the owl is a she? She is said to be wise as an owl. Look at wise. You could cipher wise as " I see double u, or two of you". If she turns her head 180 degrees to the rear and starts to walk backwards, which way would she be walking? Hun? Say wha? Her head being able to turn about is a play upon the spiral action of kundalini. Lilith being a bird means that she can **ascend,** as in she ascends up the spinal column. Her body elongates into the caduceus staff. Her wings are show at the top of the caduceus staff. There is a play upon a owl sitting on a branch. The screech of Lilith is a twofold sound. On one hand, the screeching sound when internal represents the sound of the kundalini as it ascends. On the other hand, the screeching sound is that of the orgasmic male. The huge eyes of the owl become Ida and Pangala of the kundalini coil. The mouth of the owl becomes the central path. It important to remember that the owl is a carnivore. In the case of the kundalini coil, the owl eats the mystical seed or fruit if you will.

THE FORBIDDEN FRUIT

At this point, we should talk about the forbidden fruit. Let's start out with the fruit of the trees in the garden of Eden. Is it one tree, two trees, or one tree with a common root? We know that one fruit is that of everlasting life. This is a key to our story. There is a fruit of the knowledge of " good AND evil ". This I emphasize because this is the fruit that Adam Kadmon was warned about eating! The " death " that is spoken about is that of innocence. You could think of Adam Kadmon as a " virgin " to the ways of " EVIL ". It is implied that while the mindset of Adam Kadmon could imagine " EVIL " or wrong doing, the concepts thought of would most likely be thought of as " just silly " in the long run. The concept of doing such EVIL things would even be conceptually shocking! Have you heard something on the news and begin to wonder about who could even think of such a thing. Maybe you have seen a television show or a movie and wondered about the movie. Have you ever seen a movie and in wondering about the movie asked yourself " who could have even thought of such a thing to even make a movie about it "? It is one of those type of thoughts. It is kind of when you tilt your head to the side in wonderment if you have the correct perspective upon the subject that you are viewing? I think the word that we are looking for is " bizarre "! I had planned on explaining different concepts by the modern tool called motion pictures or movies for short. Under the concept of bizarre, I would suggest going to my book store at " spiritualshock.com " and getting House Of 1,000 Corpses (Check out Great Horror Movie Quotes on YouTube). First there were books called novels that tried to demonstrate the variations in the human character. The new form of the novel is motion pictures. A motion picture can become almost like a hologram from and exterior mental perspective. Due to the nature of what a movie is, much more information can be given in a short period of time. I think of my quest to understand what a obelisk was. In my mind I could not conceive what the form was. One picture put a very quick end to that quest. Seeing the object in its intended environment also gave way to clues as to what it could be used for! The change in ones mindset is often referred to as knowledge. The concept is " to know "! From the scientific perspective, this is the difference between theory and practice. It should be noted that in most cases there is a huge difference between thinking and knowing.

IN DA KNOW

When a person thinks they know how something takes place, that is just theory. Once a person has experienced the subject at hand, they are said to have experience in said subject. This does not imply that the person can perform on an efficient level, it just means that they have experienced the subject. As when I did the kundalini exercise; I did it, but I did not know what it was that I had experienced. I had to study just to find out what it was that I had gone through. As I began to understand the parts of the event and their relationship to the whole, I became what is called " in the know "! A slang or eubonic way to put being " in the know " is called to be down with it! < Note: after saying that, " Bet " should be said, as in you had better bet it! >. If you want to get an idea about " the loss of innocence while going to a higher level, go to my book site at " spiritualshock.com " and click on " Man of Tai Chi " featuring Keanu Reeves. The Bible explains this man " being in the know " of EVIL very clearly. It was the general mindset of man to ponder and do EVIL that caused the destruction by flood sentence during the time of Noah. As a note, it seems as if for generations man worked at being as " EVIL " as he could be. The strange part is to wonder did any human decide that they were going to be as " GOOD " as possible.

FUNNY CLOUDS

Sometimes when these things come to mind, they are "kind of" funny. When I say funny, I mean that the sudden awareness or thought makes you just wonder. When I say wonder, an insight concept will make you search your mind to reanalyze the concept of concern.

I would like to talk about the concept of "coming in the clouds"! Let us just think about the concept of "coming in the clouds". Look at each word on a case by case basis. The terms are: 1) coming, 2) in, 3) the, and 4) clouds. Look at the term "coming". What is the meaning of coming? Coming implies that there is a motion of something moving from somewhere to somewhere else. The somewhere else does not imply a motion from "A" to "B". The motion could imply a transition of something from one place to another in a sequence. The sequence could be from point "A" to "B", or it could be from "F" to "K' in an "A" through "Z" sequence, the observer could be located "anywhere" from "K" through "Z" or even beyond. The concept of "anywhere" implies that the vantage point of "the seer is at or above "A". That means that "the seer" could be within the "A" through "K" circuit; or 'the seer" could be beyond "K". The concept of being beyond "K" means that the seer "could be viewing the event be either somewhere from "K" through "Z", or the vantage point could b outside of the point "Z"!

In thinking of this, the symbolic concept of the language must be taken into account. I say this because the terms of "the Sun" and "the Moon" may be used. If we think of "our" earthly example, to see something "coming in the clouds" would imply a "downward" type of motion. The concept would be like seeing a rain cloud. As the rain falls to Earth, if the viewer is standing upon the Earth, the viewer could be said to "be able to" see the rain coming in the clouds. This is the Earth viewed perspective. What about the concept of watching the rain "coming' from the grounds of the Earth upward towards the atmospheric clouds. Does that concept make any sense? In this concept, I thought of the reversed hurricane. I forget what this is called, but it I where the air is being drawn upward. When this type of storm happens at sea, the sea water is drawn upward into "the clouds". If we expand our example to a cosmic model, the concept of viewing the event from a celestial vantage point could be considered. Here is a sort of joke. Suppose "the man on the moon" is looking down upon the Earth, "the man on the moon" would be able to say that it could see the "water spout" coming in the clouds.

We need to return to the "as above, so below" type of concept. This term could imply a duality of motion within a circuit. I am thinking of the kundalini process. The duality of the system that I refer to is that the poles could be reversed. If you think of a pipe, the concept is that fluid could flow in either or more than one direction. This type of motion is often spoken of when it is stated that "the kundalini fluid current" ascends "up" the spinal column to the brain or skull. In this case, the viewer could be thought of as looking down "into" the sushumna central kundalini path from the "mystical" inner third eye. The lower "two' spheres of the human body could be thought of, in this example as being "the Earth" system. The Earth system has two spheres. The two spheres are called the Earth and the Moon. The two spheres each are said to have their own motion. In addition, it is said that the motion of the Moon sphere causes fluid movements upon the Earth "asteroid". Just as a strange note, it appears that the quest of space is also a search for another source of "water" < UNTIL THEY LEARN HOW TO MAKE IT < RAIN >>.

JEWISH MYSTICISM: PNEUMATIKOS SOMA

< BIBLE NOTES: SPIRITUAL BODIES >

< FROM BLUELETTERBIBLE.COM >

Outline of Biblical Usage: relating to the human spirit, or rational soul, as part of the man which is akin to God and serves as his instrument or organ

1. that which possesses the nature of the rational soul
2. belonging to a spirit, or a being higher than man but inferior to God
3. belonging to the Divine Spirit
   1. of God the Holy Spirit
   2. one who is filled with and governed by the Spirit of God
4. pertaining to the wind or breath; windy, exposed to the wind, blowing

KJV Translation Count — Total: 26x

The KJV translates Strongs G4152 in the following manner: spiritual (26x).

Thayer's Greek Lexicon

Lexicon : Strong's G4152 - pneumatikos

Strong's Number G4152 matches the Greek [REMOVED](pneumatikos),
which occurs 26 times in 21 versus in the Greek concordance of the KJV

Rom 1:11	For I long to see you, that I may impart unto you some spiritual [**G4152**] gift, to the end ye may be established;
Rom 7:14	For we know that the law is spiritual: G4152 but I am carnal, sold under sin.
Rom 15:27	It hath pleased them verily; and their debtors they are. For if the Gentiles have been made partakers of their spiritual things, G4152 their duty is also to minister unto them in carnal things.
1Co 2:13	**Which things also we speak, not in the words which man's wisdom teacheth, but which the Holy Ghost teacheth; comparing spiritual things G4152 with spiritual. G4152**
1Co 2:15	But he that is spiritual G4152 judgeth all things, yet he himself is judged of no man.
1Co 3:1	And I, brethren, could not speak unto you as unto spiritual, G4152 but as unto carnal, even as unto babes in Christ.
1Co 9:11	If we have sown unto you spiritual things, G4152 is it a great thing if we shall reap your carnal things?

1Co 10:3	And did all eat the same spiritual G4152 meat;
1Co 10:4	And did all drink the same spiritual G4152 drink: for they drank of that spiritual G4152 Rock that followed them: and that Rock was Christ.
1Co 12:1	Now concerning spiritual G4152 gifts, brethren, I would not have you ignorant.
1Co 14:1	Follow after charity, and desire spiritual G4152 gifts, but rather that ye may prophesy.
1Co 14:37	If any man think himself to be a prophet, or spiritual, G4152 let him acknowledge that the things that I write unto you are the commandments of the Lord.
1Co15:44	It is sown a natural body; it is raised a **spiritual G4152 body**. There is a natural body, and there is a spiritual G4152 body.
1Co 15:46	Howbeit that was not first which is spiritual, G4152 but that which is natural; and afterward that which is spiritual. G4152
Gal 6:1	Brethren, if a man be overtaken in a fault, ye which are spiritual, G4152 restore such an one in the spirit of meekness; considering thyself, lest thou also be tempted.
Eph 1:3	Blessed be the God and Father of our Lord Jesus Christ, who hath blessed us with all spiritual G4152 blessings in heavenly places in Christ:
Eph 5:19	Speaking to yourselves in psalms and hymns and spiritual G4152 songs, singing and making melody in your heart to the Lord;
Eph 6:12	For we wrestle not against flesh and blood, but against principalities, against powers, against the rulers of the darkness of this world, against spiritual G4152 wickedness in high places.
Col 1:9	For this cause we also, since the day we heard it, do not cease to pray for you, and to desire that ye might be filled with the knowledge of his will in all wisdom and spiritual G4152 understanding;
Col 3:16	Let the word of Christ dwell in you richly in all wisdom; teaching and admonishing one another in psalms and hymns and spiritual G4152 songs, singing with grace in your hearts to the Lord.
1Pe2:5	Ye also, as lively stones, are built up a spiritual[G4152] house, an holy priesthood, to offer up

spiritual [G4152] sacrifices, acceptable to God by Jesus
Christ.

1Pe2:5   Ye also, as lively stones, are built up a spiritual [G4152] house, an holy
priesthood

SEEING THE GLORY: THE SPIRITUAL BODY

Seeing the glory like Moses at mountain < from the back, get it? >.

"Young's"
24 (http://bible.cc/john/4-24.htm) God is a Spirit, and those worshiping Him, in spirit and truth it
doth behoove to worship.'
You are correct. At the resurrection we will be given spiritual bodies [I Corinthians 15:50-52].
But....in the mean time mankind has a "Spirit" within him.
Oh. absolutely. The spirit is clothed here on earth by our earthly body < this is our jail bird suite
>. It is clothed in heaven by the heavenly body.
Young's: 45 (http://bible.cc/1_corinthians/15-45.htm) so also it hath been written, 'The first man
Adam became a living creature,' the last Adam is for a life-giving spirit,
44 (http://bible.cc/1_corinthians/15-44.htm) it is sown a natural body, it is raised a spiritual body;
there is a natural body, and there is a spiritual body;
These two bodies do not occur at the same time.
Correct, the spiritual comes AFTER the earthly.
Young's: [Job 32:8]
8 (http://bible.cc/job/32-8.htm) Surely a spirit is in man, And the breath of the Mighty One Doth
cause them to understand.
It is this spirit that distinguishes us from other "Living Souls" (animals/Nephesh).
Well, along with the fact we walk upright on two legs, communicate symbolically and have
opposing thumbs.
Young's: 28 (http://bible.cc/matthew/10-28.htm) 'And be not afraid of those killing the body, and
are not able to kill the soul, but fear rather Him who is able both soul and body to destroy in
gehenna.
Well....this passage certainly proves that men can kill the body but only Yahweh can kill the

soul.

It also shows that we have both, a body to clothe the soul and of course , a soul. 2 Cor 4:2-4 speaks of it too.

Soul is rendered "life" and in this passage can only mean "Eternal" life. Mankind can take the life of another and we know that "Souls" do indeed die [Ezekiel 18:4-20]....but they (according to the passage) must be the same as [Romans 6:23] tells us.....death is the wage of sin....but eternal life is a gift.

The word soul, many times in the bible, is referring only to a person. However, the soul can also be the inner self of the person the part of us which lives on after physical death. 2 Peter 1 tells of PETER walking away from his earthly body and being aware of existence.

13 I think it is right to refresh your memory as long as I live in the tent of this body, 14 because I know that I will soon put it aside, as our Lord Jesus Christ has made clear to me. 15 And I will make every effort to see that after my departure you will always be able to remember these things.

A parallel passage is [Luke 12:4-5]

(I have to switch from Young's, I find it difficult to unravel what they are talking about as I use it so seldom.)

4 "I say to you, My friends, do not be afraid of those who kill the body and after that have no more that they can do. 5 But I will warn you whom to fear: fear the One who, after He has killed, has authority to cast into hell; yes, I tell you, fear Him!

Here is the Greek:

I'm not able to read Greek or Hebrew. I know a few key words and that's it!

Same word (removed) translated in Revelation as "Soul" but translated "Lives" in I John.

That is the Hebrew definition of "Soul".....animal life....air breathing creatures!

New Testament: [Acts 2:41][Acts 7:14][Acts 27:37][I Peter 3:20]

Old Testament: [Genesis 12:5][Genesis 46:18-22][Genesis 46:25-27][Exodus 1:5][Joshua 10:28-32][Joshua 10:35-39][Joshua 11:11]

Here is a meaning of soul from Strongs which I use to understand the word in that context in the bible.

c) the soul as an essence which differs from the body and is not dissolved by death (distinguished from other parts of the body)

The Ancient Greeks developed the idea of "Immortality of the "Soul". You do not find those words together at any place in scripture...... "Immortal Soul". The concept is totally pagan. It entered early Christianity through some of the ECFs who were influenced by the Greeks....and their customs. It is not Biblical in the slightest.

It is a general understanding developed by putting a lot of the NT together. I think the immortal soul is understood by a majority of Christians.

Adam was created on the eighth day - HubPages

> www.woman54.hubpages.com/hub/eighth-day-creation   Cached

> All my life, I believed what most people believe, that Adam was created on the sixth day. After some time of serious Bible study, I finally saw the light.

1. God Created Evolution: Cain, His City, and His Descendants

   headlyvonnoggin.hubpages.com/hub/God-Creation-Evolution...   Cached

   http://newwoman54.hubpages.com/hub/eighth-day-crea. A hub you might be interested in. HeadlyvonNoggin 14 months ago from Texas Hub Author. Thank you for sharing that ...

2. what race was Adam

   upuwas.keep.pl/what-race-was-adam.php   Cached

   There are many things in God's word that we have not .
   http://newwoman54.hubpages.com/hub/eighth-day-creation. Biblical Research Institute ...

3. Did Neanderthal man come from Adam? [Archive] - Christian ...

   forums.carm.org/vbb/archive/index.php/t-101738.html   Cached

good day, there is a doctrine called the 8 day man.
http://newwoman54.hubpages.com/hub/eighth-day-creation basically it states God
created all the races ...

4. http://newwoman54.hubpages.com/hub/eighth-day-creation

dir.abroadeducation.com.np/Eighth_Day_Creation   Cached

Eighth Day Creation: All website links, descriptions, review related to Eighth Day
Creation. The best recommendations for Eighth Day Creation

INTERESTING INTERNET " CHRISTIAN DISCUSSION FORUMS " – TOPIC:
DID NEANDERTHAL MAN COME FROM ADAM?

I add this just to record some of what people are talking about. In reality, I found one
comment very funny, so that was also a reason why I recorded this. On second thought, I have
sixty eight pages to include which are done. I now feel that I am going to " control alt delete ".
Poof, it's gone!

RAIDERS OF THE LOST ARK PROBLEM

I have seen the movie Raiders Of The Lost Ark several times. Every time that I saw the
movie I thought about its metaphysical meanings. What it is that is so important is that the
movie seems to try to show and religious subject as close as it could be based upon the religions
own rule on idolatry. I found that seeing the transitions of the religion was very helpful. At the
end of the movie a question is subconsciously asked. In a way, the question being asked without
words is " what's in the boxes " ? On one hand you might think that it is other artifacts such as "
idols ". We start out with a guess of there are " idols " in the boxes. We guess this because we
see an idol at the beginning of the movie. The movie shows that the ark is active. We see the
scene with the rats and the wood crate being burned from the inside out. This should have

peaked one's awareness to know that whatever was in the box was active. Remember that this happened before The Ark was opened to be tested. One would have to conclude that based upon what is known about the religion in question that The Ark would react towards idols being around it. This could be concluded based upon what is " known " about the religion in question. I think the technical concept would be that thy shall not have any god or gods beside The Lord your God. Now the question would be if there cannot be idols and artifacts from other religions around The Ark, what might be in the crates? I guess that I should state that the religion in question is Judaism. There might be other relics in the crates. In trying to think about powerful religious items in Judaism, I am thinking the The Ark would be one of, if not the most powerful relic of the Judaism religion. What could be in all of those crates? That's a lot of crates! There could be parts of a dismantled temple. You might even think that parts of Noah's Ark < get it > are in the crates. There is something else that may be in the crates. If you watched the movie, you were shown how serious the " subject " would be. The answer is very important especially to the Jews that believe that Jesus is The Messiah. This is very important and I know the reason why. I'm going to tell you why this is so important. The people whom are against Jesus are against the Christians having access to " the knowledge ". The question should be asked why would someone not want a group of people having access to knowledge, if the knowledge will increase the argument of the perspective to be false. Without being funny, suppose there were two groups of people. One group says that elephants cannot fly. There is another group of people that " believe " that elephants " can " fly. What makes the matter worst is that both groups claim to be experts on animals, with the major of each group is elephants. As long as there is an air of confusion, there will be no all out confrontation of the facts and truth. In reality, the difference of opinion makes the subject very interesting. One might think of this religious question as being a matter of " after life "!

REAR COVER

I respect everyone's work. Now having said that, I am tired of people writing a "new" kundalini book and adding nothing to the body of knowledge that already exists. **"The first**

statement you should make is that you have or have not opened your own kundalini coil!"
Well have you? So what, you compile data on the subject. That should be used for you to attempt to "do" if you can. This is why opening the kundalini coil is referred to as **THE GREAT WORK!** I feel that if you have nothing new or unique to add, you should not say anything at all. The body of kundalini knowledge does not need any more compilers of data and word jugglers. I think that between the ancients and myself all that needs to be said on the subject has been unless you discover some new data like I did. I am talking about books that have come forward in the last ten years. What have you added? Why do you keep using "mystical" sounding terms which are just another language. The strange thing about this science is that unless a person has done the process, you can't tell if a person is fake or not. This is based upon what I knew before I did the kundalini exercise!

AFTERLIFE: THE BOTTOM LINE

The question of there being a afterlife is the issue at hand. It seems to be very strange. In a way, the quest for the afterlife is somewhat like a nature television show that I recently viewed. It was not the first time that I had seen this show. This show had seemed very interesting to me. The show was about the hatching of sea turtles. I think the odds of survival were something like four out of one hundred will make the journey from their nest in the sand to the open waters or the beach that lead to the sea. What made the situation more complicated was that there are different levels or zones of danger.

LAST NOTE: A REST FOR GOD'S PEOPLE

From The Good News Bible: Today's English Version at Hebrews 3:7.

So then, as the Holy Spirit says,

" If you hear God's voice today,

do not be stubborn, as your

ancestors were when they

rebelled against God,

as they were that day in the

desert when they put him to

the test.

There they put me to the test and

tried me, says God,

although they had seen what I did

for forty years.

And so **I was angry with those**

people and said,

'They are always disloyal

and refuse to obey my

commands.'

I was angry and made a solemn

promise:

'They will never enter the land

where I would have given them

rest!"

JULY 11, 2014

FRANK M. CONAWAY, JR.

I hope to see you at

www.spiritualshock.com

Look up

The Apocalypse Unsealed (1910)

By James M. Pryse

www.ingramcontent.com/pod-product-compliance
Lightning Source LLC
Chambersburg PA
CBHW031302090426
42742CB00007B/561